Martha: The Cookbook

Martha
THE COOKBOOK

100 FAVORITE RECIPES, WITH LESSONS AND STORIES FROM MY KITCHEN

Martha Stewart

Photographs by Dana Gallagher

Clarkson Potter/Publishers
New York

Published in the United States by Clarkson Potter/Publishers,
an imprint of the Crown Publishing Group, a division of Penguin
Random House LLC, New York.
clarksonpotter.com

CLARKSON POTTER is a trademark and POTTER with colophon
is a registered trademark of Penguin Random House LLC.

Some recipes originally appeared in Martha Stewart Living publications.

Library of Congress Cataloging-in-Publication Data
Names: Stewart, Martha, author.
Title: Martha: The Cookbook: 100 favorite recipes, with lessons
and stories from my kitchen / by Martha Stewart.
LC record available at https://lccn.loc.gov/2023050908
LC ebook record available at https://lccn.loc.gov/2023050909
ISBN 978-0-593-13920-2
Ebook ISBN 978-0-593-13921-9

Romie © Margot Lévêque Studio
Printed in China

MARTHA STEWART LIVING OMNIMEDIA TEAM

Editorial Director Susanne Ruppert
Art Director James Maikowski
Photographer Dana Gallagher
Digital Technician Carlo Barreto
Food Editors Frances Boswell, Sarah Carey, and Thomas Joseph
Prop Stylist Lisa Wagner
Makeup Artist Daisy Toye
Librarian Kimberly Ann Dumer

Archival Photos by: William Abranowicz (page 8), Christopher Baker
(page 158), Earl Carter (pages 28, 168), Todd Eberle (page 82),
Gentl & Hyers (page 208), Guzman (page 134), Ditte Isager (page 6),
Joseph Kugliesky (page 247), Frédéric Lagrange (page 111),
Richard Phibbs (page 202), Robert Polidori (page 8), Michael Skott (page 8),
Courtesy of Martha Stewart (pages 8, 27, 33, 36, 64, 140, 195, 212,
228, 250, 260, 280), Anna Williams (pages 8, 190)

CLARKSON POTTER PUBLISHING TEAM

Editor Susan Roxborough | **Editorial Assistant** Elaine Hennig
Design Manager Stephanie Huntwork
Production Editor Terry Deal
Production Manager Kim Tyner
Copyeditors Bridget Sweet and Mark McCauslin
Indexer Elizabeth T. Parson
Publicists Jana Branson and Kate Tyler
Marketer Joey Lozada

10 9 8 7 6 5 4 3 2 1
First Edition

To my grandchildren—Jude, 13,
and Truman, 12—who have tasted and
approved so many of the recipes in
this book, and to my daughter, Alexis,
who was instrumental in instilling in
them a love of delicious food.

CONTENTS

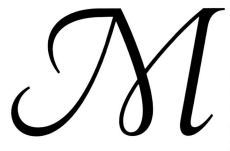

M

Y ONE HUNDREDTH BOOK IS HERE! It was so very, very exciting to be writing this. It seems like not so long ago that I was working on my first book, *Entertaining*. My then-husband, Andy, and our daughter, Alexis, flew to Utah to ski while I remained home at Turkey Hill Road in Westport, Connecticut, to put the finishing touches on that book. It was 1981. This year, the family—Alexis and her two children, Jude and Truman—went to Japan to ski and sightsee while I stayed home to focus on *Martha: The Cookbook*.

Over the course of a year, I compiled one hundred recipes that I am sure will appeal to many of you. I worked with an excellent team to photograph deliciously prepared food, cooked and styled elegantly in my home in Bedford, New York, using the very best available ingredients, much of it from my gardens. One of our most talented designers laid out the book and the typography, and I am absolutely thrilled with the results of our hard work.

It was not an easy task to choose just a hundred recipes from the thousands created over the years. I wanted to include some breakfast and brunch dishes, soups and salads, cocktails, hors d'oeuvres, dinners, garden sides, and desserts. Every night, I remembered yet another dish I thought should be added and had to restrain myself. Without a doubt, I knew I wanted to include some treasured family recipes that my mother, as a matriarch of a family of eight, made regularly. Big Martha, as she was affectionately known, appeared on my shows about forty times, demonstrating her cooking techniques—she was always a fan favorite! Then there are those everyday dishes that I eat consistently; those delicious ones that I serve my friends when entertaining; and those truly spectacular recipes I reserve for special events. I have turned to each and every one of these recipes over the years, again and again, and I hope you will, too. Also sprinkled throughout the book, within each chapter, I have included photos from my archives that are dear to me and shared stories related to them. It has been fun recalling my first trip to Paris, when Julia Child and Jacques Pépin were on my show, and making pasta with Alexis.

Please enjoy the recipes we have featured and treat yourself, your family, and your friends to a little taste of my favorites—and do not forget to start compiling your own list of favorites to hand down to your loved ones.

Martha Stewart

From top left: *My mother at twenty-seven years old and me, age two. The family home at 86 Elm Place, Nutley, New Jersey. One of my favorite portraits, taken by my dad with his fabulous Rolleiflex camera.*

From middle left: *Walking to work during my stockbroker days, circa 1970. Celebrating in Westport, Connecticut, at Turkey Hill, with my dear sister Laura, my catering staff, and my Chow Chows Max and Zuzu. Shooting the cover of my first book,* Entertaining, *which was published in 1982.*

From bottom left: *In 1999, when I had my largest number of Persian cats. The front of my Federal-style Turkey Hill farmhouse. A holiday brunch at my present home at Cantitoe Corners, in Bedford, New York, in 2010, with a group from the* Martha Stewart Living *magazine staff.*

Breakfast & Brunch

Steamed Eggs

4 large eggs, room
   temperature

   Kosher salt and freshly
   ground pepper

   Toast soldiers,
   for serving

I am always reading about eggs and their preparation, searching for new ways to cook them, to eat them, and to serve them. Because I have a plethora of eggs at all times on my kitchen counter—the many gifts bestowed on me daily by my two hundred laying hens—I use them often for breakfast, lunch, and dinner. I love traditional soft-boiled served in cups with toast and salt and pepper. I used to find that boiling in hot water would often result in hard-to-peel, cracked eggs. Journalist-chef J. Kenji López-Alt solved this problem after years of independent research, discovering that steamed eggs cooked better, peeled better, and looked better. *The New York Times* ran his results, which I read and memorized immediately; from then on, I had perfectly cooked eggs whenever I desired them. The secret is to steam room-temperature eggs in a steamer basket, covered, over boiling water—not in water! Depending on the desired doneness, this can take 6 to 12 minutes; my farm-fresh eggs require even less time, anywhere from 3 to 6 minutes is just right.

SERVES 2 TO 4

1. Fill a medium saucepan lined with a steamer basket with enough water to come just below the basket. Bring to a boil over medium-high heat. Using a large spoon, carefully place the eggs in the basket, in a single layer, and cover. Steam the eggs until set with jammy yolks, about 6 minutes.

2. Remove the eggs with the spoon, one at a time, and place each in an egg cup. To eat, use a sharp paring knife to slice off the top-third of the egg, and season with salt and pepper. Serve with toast soldiers.

Artichokes with Poached Eggs, Smoked Salmon & Hollandaise

4   **medium or large artichokes**

2   **lemons: 1 halved and 1 sliced**

     Kosher salt and freshly ground pepper

4   **medium or large eggs**

4   **thin slices smoked salmon (2 ounces total)**

     Hollandaise Sauce (recipes follow)

½   **baguette, toasted and cut into 4 slices**

The artichoke is perhaps my favorite vegetable. I love to prepare artichokes by steaming, then readying them for stuffing, filling, or just eating plain with melted butter or hollandaise. I buy only the freshest, crispest globes, leaving behind any with bruises, brown spots, or shriveled leaves or stems. If serving as a first or main course, I choose the largest chokes I can find; then prepare them carefully, using a sharp, strong knife to trim the stems and sharp kitchen shears to clip the thorny tips neatly from each leaf. For steaming the artichokes, I use a sturdy rack and set them upside down over salted boiling water in a large, covered pot, adding cut lemon for additional flavor. It's important to remove the fuzzy "choke" before serving to present the vegetable correctly. But most important of all is the cooking: To be 100 percent enjoyable, the fleshy part of each leaf has to be soft enough to scrape off with your front teeth, and the heart itself needs to be cooked just enough to cut with a knife or fork.

SERVES 4

1. Snap the tough outer leaves off the artichokes. Using a sharp knife, remove the top third from each and loosen the leaves. Cut off the stems of the artichokes, flush with the bottoms, so the artichokes stand upright. With your kitchen shears, cut off the tip of each leaf. If you're steaming a lot of artichokes, it is a good idea to soak them in acidulated water to prevent discoloration: Simply rub the cut surfaces with a lemon half and place in a pot of cold water with some additional lemon slices.

2. Fill a large stockpot with 2 inches of salted water. Set a steamer basket or a sturdy rack over the water. Stand the artichokes upside down in the basket, cover the pot, and bring to a boil. Steam the artichokes until the bottoms are tender when pierced with the tip of a knife, 30 to 40 minutes.

continued

3. Remove the artichokes from the pot and let them stand until they are cool enough to handle. Remove and discard the inner leaves, leaving trimmed outer leaves to create a flowerlike shape. Using a teaspoon, remove the fuzzy choke and any purple leaves and discard. Gently spread apart the artichoke leaves to create the desired appearance. Season with salt and pepper. Cover them to keep them warm.

4. Fill a large saucepan with 4 inches of water and bring the water to a boil. Reduce the heat to medium. When the water is barely simmering, break 1 egg into a small heatproof bowl. Gently tip the bowl to slide the egg carefully into the water. Repeat with remaining eggs. Cook until the whites are set but the yolks are still soft, 2 to 3 minutes. Lift out the eggs with a slotted spoon, briefly resting the spoon on paper towels to drain the eggs.

5. Drape 1 slice of salmon in the center of each artichoke. Spoon 1 egg on top of the salmon (be careful not to pierce the yolk). Spoon about 1 tablespoon hollandaise sauce over the top of each egg. Serve with toasted baguette and additional hollandaise on the side.

Classic Hollandaise Sauce
MAKES ABOUT 1½ CUPS

Whisk 3 large **egg yolks**, room temperature, in a large heat-proof glass bowl until they begin to turn pale, about 1 minute. Whisk in 4½ teaspoons warm water. Set the bowl over a pan of barely simmering water and heat the yolk mixture, whisking vigorously, until thickened, 2 to 3 minutes (do not overcook). Remove the bowl from the pan and whisk in 4½ teaspoons fresh **lemon juice** (from ½ a lemon). Whisking constantly, pour in 1½ sticks (¾ cup) **unsalted butter**, melted and cooled, one drop at a time at first, leaving any milky solids behind. Continue to whisk the sauce until it is thickened. Season with kosher **salt** and freshly ground **white pepper**. If you're not serving the hollandaise immediately, pour hot water from the pan into a separate (cool) pan; set the bowl on top. Keep the sauce warm, whisking occasionally, up to 30 minutes. If the sauce becomes too thick, whisk in warm water, 1 teaspoon at a time, to thin it.

Easy Hollandaise Sauce
MAKES ABOUT 1 CUP

Melt 1½ sticks (¾ cup) **unsalted butter** in a small saucepan over medium heat; let cool, about 5 minutes. Add 2 large **egg yolks** to a 2-cup liquid measuring cup. Using an immersion blender, gradually add the melted butter. Add 2 teaspoons **lemon juice** and a pinch of **cayenne**; season with kosher **salt** and freshly ground **black pepper**. (The sauce should be thick but fluid enough to drizzle from a spoon. If too thick, thin with warm water.) The sauce is best used immediately, but can be stored in a thermos for about 30 minutes.

MARTHA'S NOTE

Remember that the yolks in these sauces are not fully cooked, so they should not be prepared for pregnant women, babies, young children, the elderly, or anyone whose health is compromised.

The Perfect Omelet

1 cup fresh spinach, stemmed, washed, and drained

1 tablespoon unsalted butter

3 large eggs

Kosher salt and freshly ground pepper

¾ ounce Gruyère cheese, coarsely grated (about ¼ cup)

In the late '60s, I dined at a luncheon restaurant in New York City famous for its extraordinary omelets. Fresh eggs, lightly beaten, were quickly cooked in a heavy aluminum sauté pan designed specifically for the task by the chef, Rudolph Stanish. I bought one of his pans then, hoping my omelets would be as delicious and expertly folded as Chef Stanish's. To this day, I use that very same pan, a club hammered aluminum Rudolph Stanish Omelet Pan. In addition to being famous for his omelets, Chef Stanish is well-known for saying: "Being able to make a perfect omelet is as essential a skill for living the good life as is making a perfect cup of coffee." The perfect omelet requires not just the proper pan, but also the freshest eggs and the best unsalted butter, salt and pepper, and an assortment of delicious fillings. I usually use three eggs per omelet, poured into a preheated pan with melted butter. If you do not use the Stanish-type pan, choose a heavy stainless-steel pan or good-quality nonstick skillet and push the eggs around with a silicone spatula or flat wooden spoon. The trick is to never ever let the eggs stick—if you do, the omelet cannot be folded into thirds.

SERVES 1

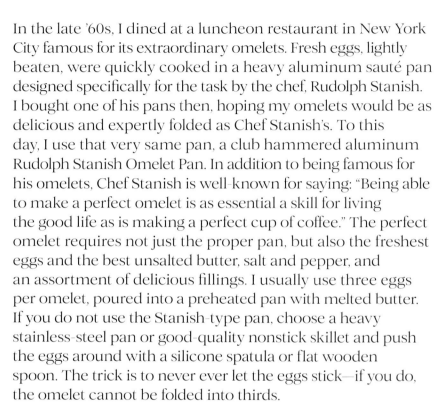

1. Sauté the spinach, with just the water clinging to it, in an 8-inch skillet over medium heat until just wilted. Transfer the spinach to a plate.

2. Wipe the skillet and heat over medium-high. (You want the pan good and hot.) Add the butter and heat until hot but not smoking. While the butter is melting, whisk the eggs in a medium bowl and season with salt and pepper. Add the whisked eggs to the skillet. Cook, gently tilting the skillet occasionally and pulling the cooked eggs away from the sides to let runny egg flow underneath, until the omelet is just set (15 to 30 seconds).

3. Add the cooked spinach and grated Gruyère. Run a spatula along one side of the omelet and gently fold over one-third. Repeat on the opposite side so that the two sides overlap in the middle. Hold the pan over a plate and slide the omelet onto the plate. Serve immediately.

Baked Frittata
(*Tortilla*)

1½ tablespoons extra-virgin olive oil

1 tablespoon unsalted butter

1 large red onion, halved and thinly sliced

Kosher salt and freshly ground pepper

2 small Yukon Gold potatoes, peeled and sliced crosswise ½-inch thick

12 large eggs

1 cup fresh spinach, stemmed, washed, and drained

5 ounces Comté cheese, finely grated (about 2 cups)

8 ounces crème fraîche

I had never had a frittata until I visited the island of Ibiza in the Spanish Balearics, while driving around Europe on my five-month honeymoon. In a tiny pension on a white sand beach, the breakfast offering was the "tortilla" of the day—one day, eggs with potatoes and onions; another day, with red peppers and onions; a third day, with spinach and potatoes. We were served a big wedge on a thick slice of oil-soaked, toasted local bread. It was the best "omelet" I had ever had. So different from the French rolled omelet or the more delicate Italian frittata, the Spanish version was thick, well-seasoned, and cooked in a hot wood-fired domed oven. I make frittatas often, using anywhere from a dozen to thirty eggs. This recipe includes onion, yellow potatoes, spinach, Comté cheese, and crème fraîche, but I vary the filling according to what I have in the garden or in the fridge. I recently altered this recipe to include whole oven-roasted shallots, sour cream, basil leaves, and cherry tomatoes. It's always delicious!

SERVES 6

1. Preheat the oven to 425°F. Heat the oil and butter in a medium stainless-steel or cast-iron pan over medium. Add the sliced onion and cook, stirring frequently, until soft and golden brown, 10 to 12 minutes. If the onion begins to stick to the pan, add 1 to 2 tablespoons water to deglaze, scraping up bits from the bottom of the pan. Remove from heat, and season with salt and pepper.

2. Fill a small pot with about 2 inches of water and add a pinch of salt. Set a steamer basket in the pot, making sure the water doesn't seep through the holes. Bring to a boil, then reduce to a rapid simmer.

Add the potatoes to the basket and steam until the potatoes are just tender when pierced with the tip of a paring knife, 8 to 10 minutes, and let cool.

3. In a bowl, whisk the eggs. Season with salt and pepper.

4. Layer the ingredients in a 2-quart baking dish: onion, potatoes, eggs, salt and pepper to taste, spinach, and cheese; repeat, finishing with dollops of crème fraîche on top. Bake until the frittata is cooked throughout, about 40 minutes. Transfer to a wire rack to let cool before serving.

Custard Egg Sandwiches

Softened unsalted
butter, for baking dish
and bread

12   large eggs

¾   cup whole milk

¼   cup heavy cream

½   teaspoon fresh thyme
leaves

Kosher salt and freshly
ground pepper

2   cups watercress, tough
stems trimmed

2   teaspoons unseasoned
rice vinegar

Shokupan (Japanese
milk bread) or other
white bread, sliced

I first ate a custard egg sandwich in Boston, at Joanne Chang's lovely Flour Bakery + Cafe. My version of the delicious classic is served on shokupan, a fluffy milk bread, cut into thick slices and lightly toasted. Trim the silky soufflé-like custard into squares the same size as the bread, and top it with watercress for a delightful crunchy contrast.

MAKES 4 TO 6 SANDWICHES

1. Preheat the oven to 300°F. Bring a kettle of water to a boil. Butter an 8-inch square baking dish. In a large bowl, whisk the eggs thoroughly. Whisk in the milk, cream, thyme, ¾ teaspoon salt, and ¼ teaspoon pepper. Pour the mixture into the prepared dish.

2. Place the dish inside a roasting pan on the center rack of the oven; add boiling water to the roasting pan to come halfway up the sides. Cover the pan with a baking sheet and bake for 40 minutes. Uncover and continue baking until the center is firm, 3 to 5 minutes more. Remove the dish from the oven and water bath, and transfer to a wire rack to cool.

3. Toss the watercress with rice vinegar in a small bowl, and season it with salt and pepper. Toast and butter the bread.

4. Cover the custard dish with a quarter baking sheet and flip it over so the dish is on top, and gently place them on a work surface. Remove the baking dish and cut the egg custard into equal pieces. Place each on a slice of bread; then top it with the watercress and a second slice of bread. Halve the sandwiches and serve.

Coddled Eggs

Extra-virgin olive oil

1 cup sliced mushrooms, such as cremini and oyster

Kosher salt and freshly ground pepper

Unsalted butter, softened, for brushing

2 tablespoons Dijon mustard

1 tablespoon honey

1 tablespoon snipped chives

6 to 12 large eggs, depending on size of coddlers

2 tablespoons heavy cream

Sharp cheddar cheese, grated

Brioche, sliced thin, for toast points

Chervil sprigs, for serving

It seems that every good host has a coddled egg recipe to use when lucky overnight guests stay for a leisurely breakfast. I received English porcelain egg coddlers when I was married, and I loved coddling eggs for my daughter and her friends in those charming dishes. I added their favorite flavorings to the carefully broken eggs in the small, buttered cups and steamed them, well covered. On a recent overnight to my friend Ham Clark's house in Virginia, I got a few tips that encouraged me to revisit these delightful eggs. Ham included a bit of mustard and honey to his concoction, and I have now amended my simpler recipe to do the same. The result? Very tasty, tender eggs steamed in a rich custard, studded with mushrooms, herbs, and cheese. You can add other fillings as you like, such as ham, sautéed onions—really, whatever your preference!

SERVES 6

1. Fill a large saucepan lined with a steamer basket with enough water to come just below the basket. Bring water to a boil over medium-high heat.

2. Meanwhile, sauté the mushrooms: Heat a medium skillet over medium. Coat the skillet with oil, and then add the mushrooms. Season with salt and pepper. Cook, stirring frequently, until browned and liquid has evaporated, about 8 minutes.

3. Brush the insides of the coddlers generously with butter. In a small bowl, mix together the mustard and honey. Add a dollop of honey mustard to each coddler. Add the sautéed mushrooms to the coddlers (about 1 tablespoon to each) and sprinkle evenly with the chives.

4. Depending on the size of the coddler, add 1 or 2 eggs. Season with salt and pepper. Add 1 teaspoon cream to each coddler (cream will surround the eggs and keep them moist). Top with grated cheese.

continued

5. Clamp or screw the coddler lids on tightly. If using ramekins or custard cups, use parchment: Cut a circle larger than the top, lightly moisten the parchment, then cover each coddler, securing it with a rubber band around the rim. Pull the edges of the parchment circle down tightly.

6. Use tongs to carefully lower the coddlers onto the steamer basket, and immediately reduce the heat to medium. Cover the pan and simmer, until the whites are just set: For a single egg, 6 to 7 minutes; for 2 eggs, simmer 7½ minutes, turn off the heat, and let stand in the steamer for 3 to 4 minutes.

7. Meanwhile, make the toast points: Preheat the broiler, with a rack 6 to 8 inches below the element. Slice the crusts off the bread, and cut each slice into quarters, to form 4 triangles. Place in a single layer on a rimmed baking sheet. Brush with oil and broil until golden at edges, 3 to 4 minutes, flipping halfway through. Transfer to a wire rack and let cool slightly.

8. Lift the coddlers from the steamer basket, remove the lids, garnish with chervil sprigs, and serve with the toast points.

CHICKENS & DUCKS AT TURKEY HILL

I PRIDE MYSELF ON spearheading, along with a few others, the trend of backyard animal husbandry in the suburbs. Shortly after moving from New York City to a four-acre property in Westport, Connecticut, my family and I made the decision to build a chicken coop and chicken yard and to fill it with egg-laying hens. Then came the ducks, the turkeys, and even some geese. Instead of selecting simple, well-known breeds, we chose blue-egg layers, Araucanas; chocolate-brown-egg layers, Marans; and other prolific egg layers, such as Cochins, Australorps, and Silkies. They were fed with organic feed, corn, and vegetable scraps. Since I was fortunate to have delicious farm-fresh specimens every day, I focused a lot on egg recipes and determining the very best ways to prepare eggs. I also discovered that using homegrown eggs in cakes, custards, and ice creams resulted in far superior products. I have had a huge chicken house complex on my property ever since—and I have never looked back.

Photo courtesy of author, circa 1972

Green Juice

1 large bunch spinach,
  washed and drained

2 celery stalks
  with leaves

1 Kirby cucumber

1 bunch fresh flat-leaf
  parsley leaves

1 small bunch fresh mint
  leaves

1 one-inch piece of fresh
  ginger, unpeeled

2 unpeeled orange wedges

My green juice has always been an essential part of my diet, and it has become an invaluable part of my quest for aging gracefully. I have developed a system on my farm in Bedford, New York, for growing healthy greens year-round—spinach, parsley, mint—and am now even cultivating cucumbers, celery, and other vegetables so my green juice will be tasty and vitamin- and mineral-laden. I credit my clear, smooth skin and shiny, thick hair and high energy level to this lightning-bolt drink, which I consume every day. I no longer include fruits and vegetables that are high in sugar, like bananas, pineapples, beets, and carrots; but I get more flavors by incorporating oranges and grapefruits with their rinds, and pomegranate seeds. I now also add a scoop of collagen, which helps with skin and bone maintenance. I have tried every type of juicer and have settled on the Breville, which extracts a lot of juice; it's also one of the easiest machines to clean. Once hooked on juicing, chances are you will stay hooked.

SERVES 2

Press all ingredients through a juicer.
Stir and serve immediately.

Making green juice in 2008, with my two French bulldogs, Francesca and Sharkey, by my side.

Homemade Yogurt with Fruit

1 gallon unhomogenized whole milk

3 to 4 tablespoons of your favorite plain whole-milk yogurt (with live, active cultures), as your starter

Serving suggestions: baked rhubarb (page 46), fresh peaches, fresh golden and red raspberries, fresh mint, and honey

I have been making my own cultured yogurt at home for a long time, but never so successfully as in the past year after I filmed a segment for my Roku show with the queen of yogurt, mother of the White Moustache brand, Homa Dashtaki. I immediately adopted Homa's techniques, and each batch I now make is silky, smooth, and creamy. (The resulting whey, after straining the basic yogurt, is beloved by all my dogs, who lap it up after dinner.) Every day, I eat a small amount of the yogurt, varying the way I serve it according to what's on hand: topped with fresh berries or baked rhubarb, mixed with cut-up fruit, pink applesauce, a spoonful of homemade jam, or grated cucumber and salt (raita), or spooned over granola—or just plain. The one essential to making yogurt is good, fresh milk, preferably unhomogenized from a reputable dairy. The starter you use is important also—I prefer the White Moustache Greek-style yogurt, refreshing my starter every month or so. I use glass or porcelain bowls, and a stainless-steel pot for heating the milk. My straining cloth is a flour sack towel, which I found works better than cheesecloth. Follow these tips and this recipe, and you're on your way!

MAKES ABOUT 1 GALLON

1. In a stainless-steel pot, bring the milk to a boil, stirring to avoid scorching it. Turn off the heat and allow the milk to cool, 35 to 45 minutes. Add the yogurt. Transfer the mixture into a very large porcelain or glass bowl, and cover it with a plate. Wrap the bowl with a warm blanket. Let it stand at room temperature for 24 hours.

2. Unwrap the bowl and refrigerate, undisturbed, for 24 hours. Strain the yogurt: Line a large bowl with a flour sack towel. Uncover the yogurt and spoon it into the towel. Pull up the corners of the towel and secure; hang it over the bowl to drain, at room temperature. Remove the yogurt from the towel after 8 to 12 hours. (Refrigerate in airtight sealed jars up to 2 weeks.) Serve with fruit, mint, and honey.

THE BERRY PATCH

Babushka'd and attired in a bathing suit and work khakis, I spent hours whenever I could in the garden—planting, weeding, and picking. I have had a large and productive garden wherever I had a house. When my then-husband, Andy; our daughter, Alexis; and I were living in New York City, we had a weekend home in Middlefield, Massachusetts, and that's where this photo was taken. We grew all sorts of things, berries included. I would peruse the seed and plant catalogs endlessly to make sure I had as many varieties of fruit and vegetables and herbs as I could possibly need for cooking and entertaining. To serve friends golden raspberries atop homemade yogurt or buttermilk ice cream was a special treat—not just for those friends but also for me! The taste difference between red raspberries and yellow is notable, by the way, and I like both equally well. But if you plan to make jam, red berries are better.

Photo courtesy of author, 1960s

Donn's Waffles with Candied Bacon

2 large eggs, separated, plus 3 large egg whites, at room temperature

1 cup unbleached all-purpose flour

¾ cup sour cream

2 tablespoons coarse cornmeal

1 teaspoon baking soda

1½ cups buttermilk

5 tablespoons unsalted butter, melted

Vegetable oil cooking spray, for waffle iron

Candied Bacon, for serving (recipe follows)

Pure maple syrup, for serving

In the 1980s, I met a fabulous family in Napa Valley, California—the Chappellet clan. Donn and Molly left Los Angeles in the late '60s and bought a beautiful piece of wine country in St. Helena. They established one of the earliest and most celebrated vineyards in the United States, and their sprawling ranch home and incredible gardens have been the subject of several books written by Molly. Entrepreneurial and handsome Donn could often be found in the family kitchen, whisking up these airy, crunchy, crispy, delectable waffles for guests and family. When I bought my home in Seal Harbor, Maine, it came equipped with five professional waffle irons, the same as Donn used, and I asked him for the recipe. What makes these extra-special and unique? The softly beaten egg whites added for lightness and the coarse stone-ground yellow cornmeal for delightful crunch. And the crispness? Easily attained by passing the hot waffle back and forth from hand to hand, to dry out the steamy surface.

SERVES 6

Candied Bacon

MAKES 12 SLICES

Preheat the oven to 350°F. Line a rimmed baking sheet with foil; then top with a wire rack on top. Arrange 12 thick-cut slices **bacon** in a single layer on the rack. Evenly sprinkle the bacon with ¼ cup granulated or brown **sugar** and ¼ teaspoon **cayenne**. Bake for 15 minutes, then flip the slices and sprinkle evenly with another ¼ cup sugar and ¼ teaspoon cayenne. Continue baking until crisp and browned, about 15 minutes more.

1. Preheat a waffle iron on the highest setting. Mix together 2 yolks, the flour, sour cream, cornmeal, and baking soda. Stir in the buttermilk, ½ cup at a time. Stir the melted butter into the batter (do not overmix).

2. Beat the 5 egg whites with a mixer on high speed until stiff peaks form. Stir half into the batter. Gently fold in the remaining whites with a silicone spatula.

3. Coat the waffle iron with cooking spray before cooking the first waffle (you don't need to repeat unless the waffles start to stick). Pour a heaping cup of batter into the center of the waffle iron (the batter should spread to the edges without overflowing). Close the lid, and cook until the waffle is golden and crisp, about 6 minutes.

4. Remove the waffle from the iron. Quickly toss the waffle between your hands to release the steam—this will help it remain crisp. Serve the waffles, with bacon and maple syrup, as they are cooked. Repeat with the remaining batter.

RISE & SHINE

This photo brings back fond memories of life in a small, crowded apartment kitchen, preparations for breakfast underway, baby Alexis nearby. I cooked so much in the early years of my marriage, always learning new recipes, trying new techniques, experimenting with new flavors. This is where I cooked every recipe in *Mastering the Art of French Cooking, Volume One,* by Julia Child, Simone Beck, and Louisette Bertholle. We ate out a bit, but not a lot. Restaurants in New York at that time tended to be either beyond our budget or inconvenient for a young couple with a baby.

Our first family apartment was on 101st Street and Riverside Drive, in a nice fifteen-story building (not the finest building by any means). Our corner apartment faced the Hudson River and south. It was six-and-a-half rooms, nicely proportioned, with high ceilings and a rent of two hundred and fifty dollars a month. Before we moved in, we sanded and stained the floors ourselves. We painted all the rooms: the living room a lovely brown, the dining room a Van Gogh yellow, our bedroom and guest room shades of gray, and the baby's room white with a beautiful blue trim. We installed a cork floor in the kitchen and baby's room, and a laundry room in the baby's bathroom. As working parents with a baby, we were thrilled to wake up with a view and go to sleep with a sunset.

In the late '60s, I had a full-time job as an institutional stockbroker, and we often had friends over for dinner. I also enjoyed making breakfast every morning. I loved baking, so I always made biscuits and muffins. Any extras would be taken to the office, where they would be devoured. My husband loved taking pictures with his Leica 35mm with real film—even when I was in curlers and a skimpy housedress!

Photo courtesy of author, 1960s

Blueberry Muffins

2 cups unbleached all-purpose flour

1½ teaspoons baking powder

½ teaspoon kosher salt

3 cups fresh blueberries

1 stick (½ cup) unsalted butter, softened

1 cup sugar, plus 1 tablespoon for sprinkling

2 large eggs

2 teaspoons pure vanilla extract

½ cup whole milk

Pinch of ground mace, for sprinkling

Perhaps my very favorite muffin is blueberry. This has been the case since I owned a little cottage in the Berkshires with my then-husband, Andy. It was there, in Middlefield, Massachusetts, where I was introduced to the very delicious highbush mountain blueberries—they are large and sweet, tart, and sour, all at the same time. Wonderful in pies, coffee cake, and pancakes, they are especially good in muffins. This muffin batter is extremely simple, flavored only with the fruit and sugar and vanilla. Sugar mixed with ground mace is sprinkled on top of the raw batter before baking for an additional crunch and unique taste. I prefer baking muffins in paper baking cups; this ensures easy removal from the pans and is also more convenient for serving. These delicious treats go fast, so I often double the recipe!

MAKES 12 MUFFINS

MARTHA'S NOTE

Tossing the blueberries with some flour mixture prevents them from sinking to the bottom of the muffins as they bake.

1. Preheat the oven to 375°F. Line a standard 12-cup muffin tin with paper liners.

2. In a medium bowl, whisk together the flour, baking powder, and salt. Working over the bowl, toss the blueberries in a fine sieve with about 1½ teaspoons of the flour mixture to lightly coat; set aside the flour mixture and the blueberries.

3. In the bowl of a stand mixer fitted with the paddle attachment, beat the butter and 1 cup sugar on medium-high speed until light and fluffy, about 3 minutes. Add the eggs, one at a time, beating until combined. Mix in the vanilla.

4. With the mixer on low speed, add the reserved flour mixture, beating until just combined. Add the milk, beating until just combined; do not overmix. Using a silicone spatula, fold in the blueberries. Divide the batter evenly among the prepared muffin cups. Mix the remaining tablespoon of sugar with the mace and sprinkle evenly on top.

5. Bake, rotating the pan halfway through, until the muffins are golden brown and a cake tester inserted in the center of one muffin comes out clean, 30 minutes. Transfer the pan to a wire rack to cool for 10 minutes before turning out muffins. Serve muffins warm or at room temperature.

Brioche French Toast

6 large eggs

1½ cups whole milk

Juice of 1 medium orange (about ¼ cup)

2 tablespoons pure vanilla extract

2 tablespoons cognac

1 tablespoon sugar, plus 3 teaspoons for sprinkling

Grated zest of 1 lemon (about 1 tablespoon)

½ teaspoon ground cinnamon

Pinch of freshly grated nutmeg

Pinch of kosher salt

6 slices brioche, 1 inch thick

⅓ cup vegetable oil, such as safflower or rice bran oil

Pure maple syrup

I am totally enamored with light, buttery, fluffy brioche. I like it sliced and toasted. I like it very thinly sliced and oven-browned into melba toasts for crème fraîche and caviar. I like it as the base for a rich fruit-studded bread pudding. But I love it most dipped in egg and milk, then fried to a light golden brown, yielding the most delectable French toast ever. As I have done with croissants, testing and grading them in every bakery in a city, I have located what I think is the very best brioche anywhere. And that anywhere is in my very own kitchen, after I have baked two or more loaves, using chef Margarita Manzke's very stellar recipe from her book, *Baking at République*. Whenever I go to her and her husband Walter's café and bakery in Los Angeles, République, I bring back as many loaves as I can. Since my trips to LA are not frequent, I have tried to master Margarita's techniques, even using the same pans and flour, to attempt to accurately re-create her incredible loaves in my kitchen. I think I have.

SERVES 6

1. Whisk together the eggs, milk, juice, vanilla, cognac, sugar, zest, cinnamon, nutmeg, and salt in a bowl. Set aside.

2. Place the bread in a shallow baking dish large enough to hold the bread slices in a single layer. Pour the egg mixture over the bread and let it soak for 10 minutes. Turn the slices over and let stand until soaked through, about 10 minutes.

3. Preheat the oven to 200°F. Place a wire rack on a baking sheet and set aside.

4. Heat the oil in a skillet over medium. Add half the bread and cook until golden brown, 2 to 3 minutes per side. Transfer the slices to the prepared baking sheet and place in the oven while you cook the remaining bread. When ready to serve, sprinkle each slice with ½ teaspoon sugar and serve with maple syrup on the side.

Popovers with Strawberry Jam

6 large eggs

2½ cups whole milk

1 teaspoon kosher salt

2½ cups unbleached
   all-purpose flour

Unsalted butter,
softened, for pans,
plus more for serving

Strawberry Jam
(recipe follows)

Popovers did not become part of my brunch repertoire until I bought my beloved home on Mount Desert Island in Maine. They are a vital part of the fabric of life on that island, served as the bread course for lunch and dinner at the Asticou Inn, and at the Jordan Pond House with lunch. Hosts serve them to their friends with jam for tea; overflowing with lobster Newburg; and filled with ham, poached eggs, spinach, and hollandaise for brunch. Huge and crispy and golden brown on the outside, they are golden yellow and hollow on the inside. Bake them in preheated popover pans and serve them hot out of the oven.

MAKES 12 POPOVERS

MARTHA'S NOTE

To sterilize jam jars before using, submerge clean jars in boiling water for 10 minutes. Use new lids and sterilize them according to manufacturer's instructions. Jars should remain in hot water until they are ready to be filled.

1. Whisk the eggs in an 8-cup liquid measuring cup. Add the milk and salt and whisk to combine. Add the flour and whisk to combine (the mixture will be lumpy). Chill overnight.

2. Place two 6-cup popover pans on a rack in lowest position in the oven. Preheat the oven to 425°F. Carefully remove the preheated popover pans from the oven and place on wire cooling racks. Generously brush each cup with butter. Fill each cup a little more than halfway with batter (be sure not to overfill cups, as popovers will rise during baking).

3. Bake for 20 minutes. (Do not open the oven door while the popovers are baking.) Reduce oven to 350°F. Bake until golden brown, about 25 minutes more. Transfer the pans to wire racks to cool in their pans for 5 minutes. Turn out the popovers. Serve warm with softened butter and homemade jam.

Strawberry Jam
MAKES ABOUT 2 PINTS

In a glass bowl, stir together 3 pounds hulled ripe **strawberries**, 5 cups **sugar**, and the juice of 1 large **lemon**. Refrigerate overnight. Transfer to a large heavy pot and bring to a simmer, stirring until the sugar has dissolved. Return to the bowl, cover, and refrigerate overnight again. The next day, strain the syrup into a large heavy stockpot; reserve the berries. Bring the syrup to a boil, then cook until a thermometer registers 221°F. Add the berries back in and boil for 5 minutes more, skimming any foam as needed. Pour the jam into hot sterilized jelly jars. Let cool completely, cover, and refrigerate up to 2 weeks, or freeze up to 6 months.

Orange-Scented Currant Scones

1 cup dried currants

¼ cup Grand Marnier

2 tablespoons grated orange zest

2 cups cake flour, sifted

1½ cups unbleached all-purpose flour, plus more for dusting

6 tablespoons granulated sugar

5 teaspoons baking powder

1 teaspoon kosher salt

1 stick (½ cup) cold unsalted butter, cut into small pieces

1 cup heavy cream

1 large egg plus 1 large egg yolk (reserve 1 egg white for egg wash)

Coarse sanding sugar, for sprinkling

Crème fraîche, for serving

Baked rhubarb, for serving (optional)

In the 1980s, I traveled quite extensively on book tours. On these tours, I would visit three or four cities to give talks and promote a new book. On one trip, to Jackson, Mississippi, I tasted some delicious orange-scented scones at a tea given for me at the home of DeRo Puckett. I went home and tried to duplicate the taste, soaking the currants in Grand Marnier and adding lots of orange zest to a cream-and-butter-infused dough. The result? Perfection. Cut into small, fluted-edged rounds and brushed with egg white and topped with sanding sugar, these tasty, flaky confections can be eaten at breakfast, for dessert, or, of course, at a tea party. And, by the way, currants are tiny raisins—they are not dried currant berries but, instead, dried Champagne grapes called Black Corinth grapes. They can be found anywhere regular raisins are sold.

MAKES ABOUT 20 SCONES

1. In a small bowl, combine the currants, Grand Marnier, and orange zest. Allow the fruit to plump, for at least 1 hour and up to overnight in the refrigerator.

2. Preheat the oven to 350°F. Line a baking sheet with parchment.

3. In a large bowl, whisk together the cake flour, all-purpose flour, granulated sugar, baking powder, and salt. Transfer half the flour mixture to a food processor. Add the butter and pulse several times to combine. Do not overprocess; some butter pieces should remain the size of large peas, while other pieces will be smaller. Add the contents of the food processor back to the bowl with the dry ingredients. Stir to combine.

4. In a small bowl, whisk to combine the cream, egg, and egg yolk. Create a well in the middle of the flour mixture and gradually add the cream mixture. Using a large spatula or wooden spoon, draw the dry ingredients over the wet ingredients, being sure to scrape from the bottom of the bowl to incorporate the dry crumbs. Add the plumped fruit and gently mix. Do not overwork the dough.

continued

5. Turn the dough out onto a lightly floured work surface. Pat into a narrow rectangle about 1 inch thick. With the short side facing you, fold the rectangle into thirds like a business letter. Turn the dough a quarter turn clockwise, so the flap opening faces right, like a book. This is the first turn.

6. With a rolling pin or your hands, gently pat into another narrow rectangle, about 1 inch thick. Repeat folding and turning process to complete a second turn.

7. Using lightly floured hands, pat the dough out into a 1¼-inch-thick rectangle. Cut out rounds, spaced as closely together as possible, using a floured 2-inch round biscuit cutter. The dough may be rerolled once, and additional rounds may be cut out.

8. Transfer the rounds to the prepared baking sheet, about 1½ inches apart. Brush with the egg white and sprinkle with sanding sugar. Bake until golden brown, 20 to 25 minutes. Let cool 15 minutes on a wire rack before serving. Serve with crème fraîche and baked rhubarb, if desired.

Baked Rhubarb

I grew up loving the rhubarb from my father's garden, stewed by Mom on the top of the stove with plenty of sugar. When I had my own garden, and my own lovely rhubarb patch, I started cooking this sour but flavorful vegetable in a buttered dish in the oven, at 375°F until it was tender. I found that it required less sugar and the stalks retained their shape much better. And red rhubarb looked so beautiful cooked like this.

Soups & Salads

Beet Soup

2 pounds red beets (about 10 small beets), reserving stems and greens

¼ cup plus 1 tablespoon white vinegar

1 teaspoon sugar

Kosher salt and freshly ground pepper

3 tablespoons olive oil

3 green onions, finely chopped

2 shallots, finely chopped

3 tender inner stalks of celery, finely chopped (about 1 cup)

1 medium carrot, chopped

1 garlic clove, minced

4 cups Homemade Vegetable Stock (page 288) or store-bought

Sour cream, for serving

Finely chopped fresh dill, for serving

I have been eating and making beet soup for many, many years. It's part of my Polish family heritage. My grandparents, who were born in rural Poland and immigrated to America in the early 1900s, brought with them traditions and recipes, borscht among them. There are quite a few versions of this tasty and colorful soup, and this one—best made with small beets just pulled from the garden and the freshest vegetables you can find—is my favorite. Dolloped with sour cream and garnished with fresh dill, it's rich in flavor, easy to make, and hearty enough to be served as a main course for lunch. The recipe is flexible; often I alter the vegetable ingredients, adding more carrots, or white turnips, small potatoes, even different-colored beets. If you prefer, it can also be made into a meat-based soup by adding braised beef cubes and beef broth.

SERVES 6

1. Set a steamer basket in a large pot. Fill it with enough water to come just below the basket. Bring the water to a boil. Place the beets in the basket and reduce heat to a simmer. Cover and cook until tender, 30 to 35 minutes; let cool then peel and coarsely grate. Toss 1 cup grated beets with the vinegar, sugar, and 1 teaspoon salt to pickle the beets.

2. Heat 2 tablespoons oil in a large saucepan. Add the green onions, shallots, ½ teaspoon salt, and pepper to taste, and sauté until the vegetables begin to soften, 6 to 8 minutes.

3. Finely chop enough of the reserved beet stems and greens to yield 1½ cups. Add the beet stems and greens, celery, carrot, garlic, and remaining 1 tablespoon oil, and sauté until the vegetables begin to soften, 6 to 8 minutes. Add the pickled beet mixture, remaining grated beets, the stock, and 1 teaspoon salt to the skillet. Bring to a simmer and cook until the vegetables are tender, about 5 minutes. Season with salt and pepper to taste. Serve with sour cream and chopped fresh dill.

Mushroom Soup

4 ounces dried mushrooms, such as Polish borowik, porcini, or cèpes

2 quarts Homemade Beef Stock (page 286), Homemade Vegetable Stock (page 288), or store-bought

5 celery stalks, finely chopped

1 large onion, finely chopped

5 carrots, coarsely chopped, or 1 bunch baby carrots (about 10), peeled and quartered lengthwise

¼ pound white button mushrooms, sliced

¼ pound shiitake mushrooms, sliced

½ cup orzo

Kosher salt and freshly ground pepper

Sour cream, for serving

Fresh flat-leaf parsley, coarsely chopped, for serving

Coarsely chopped fresh dill, for serving

For as long as I can remember, our family had a delicious Polish mushroom soup on the table for big holidays—Easter, Thanksgiving, and Christmas. My mother, affectionately called Big Martha, prided herself on her version, fragrant with dried porcini, or cèpes, imported from Poland. In later years, when "umami" entered the lexicon of chefs, we joked with Mom that her soup was the finest example of that elusive quality. For this recipe, a well-made beef stock is essential; prepared ahead and frozen in quart containers, rich homemade stocks turn soup-making into a simple task, resulting in the most flavorful of dishes.

SERVES 6

1. Rinse the dried mushrooms. Place them in a bowl and cover them generously with boiling water. Let them soak to rehydrate, stirring occasionally, for about 1 hour. Lift out the mushrooms, squeezing out any liquid, and set aside. Pour the soaking liquid through a fine-mesh sieve into a large bowl.

2. In a large pot, bring the soaking liquid and the stock to a simmer over medium-high. Add the celery, onion, and carrots. Chop the hydrated mushrooms into ¼-inch pieces and add them to the soup, along with the sliced white button mushrooms and shiitake mushrooms.

3. Cover the pot, reduce the heat to medium-low, and cook the soup until the vegetables are tender, about 1 hour. Uncover the pot and raise the heat to high. Bring the soup to a boil, stirring, and add the orzo. Reduce the heat to a gentle boil, stirring occasionally to prevent the pasta from sticking, and cook the orzo until al dente, another 6 to 8 minutes. Season with salt and pepper.

4. Serve the soup topped with a dollop of sour cream and chopped fresh parsley and dill.

Fresh Pea Soup

1 tablespoon unsalted butter

1 tablespoon extra-virgin olive oil

1 leek, white and light green parts only, sliced and washed well

1 yellow onion, diced

4 cups Homemade Vegetable Stock (page 288) or store-bought

5 cups shelled green peas

1 cup fresh spinach leaves, washed and drained

Kosher salt and freshly ground pepper

½ cup crème fraîche

Fresh herbs, such as cilantro or mint, for serving

I grow a lot of peas, and I often make soup with garden shell peas as well as with their pods. This simple, delicate soup uses only a few ingredients and just four vegetables: peas, leek, spinach, and onion. This recipe was inspired years ago, when I was perusing a battered cookbook in my library, written by Elizabeth David, an English contemporary to my mentor at the time, Julia Child. Most of her recipes were just short paragraphs—no step-by-steps and very few measurements—with just a few simple descriptive sentences. Everything I made from that book was delicious, but especially the soups. This one starts with a well-made vegetable stock (homemade is best). Enriched with a bit of crème fraîche and garnished with a sprig of herbs, a cup or a bowl will delight, especially if the peas come from your very own garden.

SERVES 6 TO 8

1. Melt the butter and oil in a large pot over medium-low heat. Add the sliced leeks and diced onion, and cook until tender, 8 to 10 minutes.

2. Add the vegetable stock, increase the heat to medium-high, and bring to a boil. Add the peas and cook until they are tender, about 5 minutes. Add the spinach, 2 teaspoons salt, and freshly ground pepper to taste, and continue to cook for 2 minutes. Remove from the heat and allow to cool slightly.

3. Carefully transfer the soup to a blender, working in batches if needed, and puree until smooth. Transfer the soup to a large bowl to cool. Just before serving, whisk in the crème fraîche. Serve garnished with fresh herbs.

Potato-and-Buttermilk Soup

2 pounds new potatoes

1 tablespoon unsalted butter

1 tablespoon extra-virgin olive oil

4 small onions, thinly sliced

3 cups cold buttermilk

Kosher salt and freshly ground pepper

Fresh dill, coarsely chopped, for serving

Depending on your point of view, this soup of hot boiled potatoes, cold buttermilk, caramelized onions, and fresh dill could be described as a humble farmer's lunch or as a sophisticated assemblage of incredibly simple, delicious ingredients. Either way, it's one of the best ways to "drink" a glass of buttermilk, which is my favorite milk. According to my family's lore, a version of this soup originated on Polish farms, where the basic ingredients could usually be found in the larder, even when there was nothing else. It's absolutely lovely as is, but sometimes I add a few crispy tidbits of sautéed bacon or even a tablespoon of caviar.

SERVES 4

1. Place the potatoes in a steamer basket. Fill a large pot with 1 to 2 inches of water. Set the basket in the pot. Bring the water to a simmer, cover, and steam the potatoes until they are tender and easily pierced with a knife, 20 to 30 minutes.

2. While the potatoes cook, heat the butter and oil in a medium skillet over high. Add the onions, reduce the heat to medium, and sauté until golden brown and slightly caramelized, 10 to 12 minutes.

3. When the potatoes are cool to the touch, use a paring knife to remove a decorative band of peel from the center of each potato. Divide the potatoes among four soup bowls and pour ¾ cup buttermilk into each bowl. Top with the caramelized onions, season with salt and pepper, and garnish with dill before serving.

Leek-and-Fennel Soup

8 leeks, white and light green parts only

3 tablespoons unsalted butter

2 yellow onions, finely chopped

6 fennel bulbs, finely chopped

Kosher salt and freshly ground pepper

6 cups Homemade Vegetable Stock (page 288) or store-bought

FOR THE CROUTONS

½ (1-pound) loaf day-old bread (such as brioche), crusts removed and cut into ¼-inch cubes

3 tablespoons extra-virgin olive oil

1 tablespoon unsalted butter, melted

Kosher salt and freshly ground pepper

Chervil sprigs, for serving

I have made so many versions of leek soup—leek and potato, leek and carrot, leek and watercress, leek and spinach—but this recipe is my favorite, hands down. The delicate, buttery flavor of leeks combined with the mild, anise-like flavor of fennel creates a delicious soup that can be served in a cup for a light lunch or in a flat soup plate as an elegant starter at a formal dinner party. To attain a desirable, velvety texture, I use a Vitamix blender and then pass the soup through a medium-mesh sieve. For garnish, tiny croutons cut from thin slices of buttery brioche, lightly toasted in the oven, and topped with chervil sprigs or chive blossom flowers make for a lovely finishing touch.

SERVES 6 TO 8

1. Clean the leeks thoroughly: Place in a large bowl of cold water; stir and let stand for 5 minutes. Lift out leeks, discard water, and rinse out bowl; repeat as necessary. Transfer the leeks to paper towels to drain. Finely chop.

2. Meanwhile, melt the butter in a large pot over medium-low heat. Sauté the onions, stirring occasionally, until softened and translucent, about 10 minutes.

3. Add the chopped leeks and fennel and cook over medium-high heat until the vegetables are tender, about 15 minutes. Season with 2 teaspoons salt and a pinch of pepper. Add the vegetable stock and bring to a boil; reduce the heat and simmer for 20 minutes.

4. Meanwhile, make the croutons: Preheat the oven to 350°F. On a rimmed baking sheet lined with parchment, toss the bread cubes with the olive oil, melted butter, 1 teaspoon salt, and ½ teaspoon pepper. Bake in a single layer until the croutons are toasted and crisp, 12 to 15 minutes, tossing halfway through.

5. Carefully transfer the vegetable soup to a blender, working in batches if needed, and puree until smooth. Adjust the soup's consistency with vegetable stock, if necessary. Season with salt and pepper to taste. Top with croutons and chervil before serving.

Orange, Yellow & Red Gazpachos

3 large orange or yellow tomatoes, coarsely chopped

2 orange or yellow bell peppers, seeded, deribbed, and coarsely chopped

1 onion, coarsely chopped

6 to 9 small celery stalks, coarsely chopped

1 English cucumber, peeled, seeded, and coarsely chopped

⅓ cup white balsamic vinegar (or to taste)

2 teaspoons kosher salt, plus more to taste

1 teaspoon hot sauce, such as Tabasco (or to taste)

1 teaspoon sugar, or to taste

At the farm in Bedford and in my kitchen garden in Maine, I grow as many types of tomatoes as I can, planting seeds that I have collected on my travels and new types that I read about in the many seed catalogs I peruse every winter. There has been a huge influx of interest in growing different colors of tomatoes—big yellow and orange tomatoes have become very popular, and the reds are now dark burgundy, green striped, and even pink in color. For my last gazpacho and paella cookout party, on my terrace in Maine, we served three beautiful and tasty gazpachos made from some of the delicious tomatoes we harvested in the garden. Each was made using my classic red recipe and each had some very subtle differences due primarily to the acidity of the tomatoes. When making gazpacho, it is important to use the ingredients called for and not to scrimp on the seasonings and herbs.

EACH SERVES 6 TO 8

Orange or Yellow Gazpacho

1. Put all the ingredients into a large bowl. Add ¾ cup water and stir until combined. Cover and let marinate in the refrigerator overnight, or up to 2 days.

2. Working in batches, pulse all the ingredients in a food processor or blender until mostly smooth. Taste and add more salt, Tabasco, and sugar, if needed, to achieve a tangy and bright flavor. Serve chilled.

continued

5 tomatoes, cored and
   cut into quarters

1 cucumber, peeled,
   seeded, and cut into
   1-inch pieces

3 celery stalks, cut into
   $\frac{1}{2}$-inch pieces

1 red onion, cut into
   $\frac{1}{2}$-inch dice

2 red bell peppers, seeded,
   deribbed, and cut into
   $\frac{1}{2}$-inch dice

$\frac{1}{2}$ jalapeño chile, minced
   (ribs and seeds removed
   for less heat, if desired)

2 garlic cloves, minced

$\frac{1}{4}$ cup chopped fresh
   flat-leaf parsley

$\frac{1}{4}$ cup chopped fresh
   cilantro

$\frac{1}{4}$ cup red wine vinegar

$\frac{1}{4}$ cup extra-virgin olive oil

$\frac{1}{4}$ cup ketchup

1 tablespoon kosher salt,
   plus more to taste

1 teaspoon hot sauce, such
   as Tabasco (or to taste)

   Halved cherry tomatoes
   and cilantro sprigs,
   for serving (optional)

Red Gazpacho

1. Put all the ingredients, except the garnishes, in a large bowl. Add 1 cup water and stir until combined. Cover and let marinate in the refrigerator overnight, or up to 2 days.

2. Working in batches, process the soup in a food processor or blender until the vegetables are mostly smooth. Season with additional salt and served chilled. Top with cherry tomatoes and cilantro sprigs, if desired.

MARTHA'S NOTE

For sit-down lunches or dinners, I serve gazpacho in shallow cut-crystal soup bowls, with a garnish of herbs and halved cherry tomatoes. When entertaining a large group, I often offer the cold soup in small glasses.

GROWING GREENS

Among the wonders of my very earliest gardens, plotted carefully to maximize the sunlight and have a pleasingly organized, symmetrical layout, were the rows upon rows of lush, beautiful lettuce. So abundant were the leafy greens—and fast-growing—that I quickly had more than enough to keep my family and our friends and neighbors well supplied for salads throughout the spring and summer. I delighted in those greens and still do. Now I keep a good supply of fresh vegetables and salad greens year-round by cultivating them in a greenhouse. I had it constructed several years ago next to the equipment barn on my farm in Bedford; it was inspired by Eliot Coleman, an expert in four-season farming.

I rarely have a dinner that is not accompanied by a salad. There is something so fresh and delicious about a well-dressed mound of garden-fresh lettuces or other greens. The gardens I grow always have various types of greens—mesclun, arugula, butter lettuce, romaine, salad bowl, spinach, and chicories of red, green, white, and pink. All these make wonderful salads for every lunch and dinner. And learning how to make a good dressing is not hard; it is all about the ingredients, which is why I have two shelves of my kitchen pantry filled with the very best oils and vinegars I can find. Wherever I go, I visit shops in search of local olive oil, special vinegar, and delicious salts and peppercorns from all over the world. The proportion of oil to acid is especially important, and I use a ratio of two parts oil to one part acid (primarily vinegar), whisked or shaken with two tablespoons of fresh Dijon mustard. Finely minced shallots add a wonderful taste, as does a squeeze of citrus right before serving.

Photo courtesy of author, 1970s

Alexis's Chopped Salad

Kosher salt

2 ears of corn, shucked

Pinch of sugar

½ pound green beans, trimmed

½ pound yellow wax beans, trimmed

4 plum tomatoes, seeded and cut into ¼-inch pieces

1 pint cherry tomatoes, halved

1 small yellow bell pepper, seeded, deveined, and cut into ¼-inch pieces

1 small red bell pepper, seeded, deveined, and cut into ¼-inch pieces

1 small purple bell pepper, seeded, deveined, and cut into ¼-inch pieces

1 English cucumber, peeled, seeded, and cut into ¼-inch pieces

1 small red onion, peeled, cut into ¼-inch pieces, and soaked in ice water

1 medium jalapeño chile, seeded, deveined, and finely chopped

¾ cup whole cilantro leaves

2 tablespoons unseasoned rice vinegar

2 tablespoons extra-virgin olive oil

1 teaspoon freshly ground black pepper

Radicchio leaves, such as Variegato di Lusia, for serving

One of my favorite salads to look at, as well as to eat, is my daughter Alexis's chopped salad. Each time she makes it, she tries to include at least ten different vegetables, and thus it is easier for summer preparation than winter, when farm stands and gardens are full of endless ingredients. Consider the list here a starting point. I change my version as my garden changes—it might also include three colors of string beans, several kinds of corn, and red, yellow, white, and striped beets. I sometimes serve this with a fancy grilled cheese sandwich for a luncheon or as a first course for a more elaborate dinner.

SERVES 12

1. Prepare an ice bath. Bring a medium saucepan of salted water to a boil. Add the corn and sugar, and blanch the corn until tender, about 6 minutes. Remove the corn from water and plunge immediately into the ice bath. When the corn is thoroughly cooled, remove it from the ice bath. Using a sharp knife, remove the kernels from cobs. Transfer the kernels to a large bowl.

2. Add the green and yellow beans to the boiling water. Blanch them until tender, about 1 minute. With a slotted spoon, remove the beans from the water and plunge immediately into the ice bath. When the beans are thoroughly cooled, transfer them to a colander to drain. Cut the beans into ¼-inch pieces and add to the bowl with corn.

3. Add the tomatoes, bell peppers, cucumber, onion, jalapeño, and cilantro leaves. Stir to combine. Add the vinegar, oil, black pepper, and 1 teaspoon salt. Toss to combine. Taste and adjust for seasoning. Keep the salad chilled until ready to serve over radicchio leaves.

Cold Mussel Salad

FOR THE PICKLED RED ONIONS

- 2 small red onions, thinly sliced
- 1 cup distilled white wine vinegar
- 2 tablespoons sugar
- 1 tablespoon kosher salt

FOR THE MUSSEL SALAD

- 3 pounds mussels, scrubbed and debearded
- Kosher salt and freshly ground pepper
- 3 tablespoons crème fraîche
- ½ teaspoon celery seeds
- 1 small bulb fennel, thinly sliced
- Grated zest and juice of 1 lemon
- Parsley sprigs, for serving

FOR THE HERB BAGUETTE

- 1 stick (½ cup) unsalted butter, melted
- ½ cup chopped mixed herbs, such as fresh curly parsley and chives
- 1 baguette, cut into ¾-inch slices
- 1 garlic clove, cut in half

This salad brings back fond memories of the lunches I shared with my stockbroker colleagues, at a small French bistro in the West Village called La Petite Ferme. Cold mussels in a rich mustardy vinaigrette were served in a big wooden salad bowl. We ate this salad with crusty French baguettes still warm from the oven, which we used to sop up the dressing. Delicious! I've dressed up that salad a bit with quick-pickled red onion, thinly sliced fennel bulb, crème fraîche, and celery seeds. The mussels must be steamed open, removed from their shells, and cooled. Use the cleanest, freshest mussels you can find; I prefer smaller plump mussels. And don't forget the baguette!

SERVES 2 TO 4

1. Make the pickled red onions: Place the onions in a medium heatproof bowl. Bring the vinegar, sugar, and salt to a boil in a saucepan; pour over the onions. Let cool completely. Refrigerate, covered, for at least 2 hours and up to 1 month. (Note: You'll be using 1 teaspoon pickling liquid for step 4.)

2. Make the mussel salad: Put the mussels and ½ cup water in a large skillet. Season with 2 teaspoons pepper. Cover and cook over high heat, stirring once, until the mussels open, 2 to 3 minutes. (Discard any unopened mussels.)

3. Transfer the mussels to a serving bowl. Season with 2 teaspoons pepper. Let cool and remove the mussels from the shells. (Discard the shells.) Transfer the mussels to the refrigerator to chill.

4. In a medium bowl, whisk together the crème fraîche, 1 teaspoon pickling liquid, the celery seeds, and salt to taste. Add the chilled mussels. Toss well to combine, cover, and refrigerate for 30 minutes.

5. In a small bowl, combine the sliced fennel, lemon zest, and lemon juice. Season with salt and pepper. Arrange the fennel and mussels on a serving dish. Top with the pickled red onions and parsley sprigs.

6. Make the herb baguette: Mix together the butter and herbs. Broil the bread until lightly toasted, flipping halfway through, 2 to 3 minutes. Remove and rub with garlic; then brush with herb butter. Return to the broiler until crisp and golden brown and butter is sizzling, 3 to 4 minutes. Serve on the side of the cold mussel salad.

Niçoise Salad

⅔ cup extra-virgin olive oil

Juice of 2 lemons
(about 6 tablespoons)

2 tablespoons Dijon
mustard

1 shallot, finely chopped

1 tablespoon capers, finely
chopped

2 teaspoons anchovy paste

Kosher salt and freshly
ground pepper

4 large eggs

½ pound haricots verts,
stem ends trimmed

2 teaspoons unseasoned
rice vinegar

8 baby potatoes

2 teaspoons dry vermouth

1 head of red leaf lettuce,
leaves removed, washed
well, and spun dry

1 head of Boston lettuce,
leaves removed, washed
well, and spun dry

½ pint red cherry
tomatoes, halved

½ pint yellow cherry
tomatoes, halved

3 (6-ounce) jars imported
tuna in olive oil, such as
Ortiz, drained

½ cup niçoise olives

When I'm at my home on Mount Desert Island, I enjoy dining on the elegant, pink granite western terrace, and one of my preferred lunches is a salad niçoise. I do not use seared fresh tuna steak but rather oil-cured tuna from Italy, found in gourmet markets. The hard-cooked eggs in this salad should have jammy yellow-orange yolks, and the potatoes should be steamed, soaked with a bit of vermouth, and dressed in the rich vinaigrette before serving. Fresh haricots verts, thin French string beans, should be boiled in salted water until tender, chilled in ice water, and then drained and dressed before adding to the salad. It is the perfect luncheon salad.

SERVES 8

1. In a medium bowl, whisk together the oil, lemon juice, mustard, shallot, capers, and anchovy paste. Season with salt and pepper. Set aside.

2. Fill a medium saucepan lined with a steamer basket with enough water to come just below the basket. Bring to a boil over medium-high heat. Using a large spoon, carefully place the eggs in the basket, in a single layer, and cover. Steam the eggs until set with jammy yolks, about 6 minutes. Let cool completely; then peel and halve. Set aside.

3. Prepare an ice bath. Fill a medium saucepan with cold salted water and bring to a boil. Cook the haricots verts until tender, 2 to 3 minutes. Immediately transfer the beans, with a slotted spoon, to the ice bath. Drain well and pat dry. Drizzle with the rice vinegar. Season with salt and pepper. Set aside.

4. Prepare another ice bath. Place the potatoes in a medium pot and cover with cold salted water. Bring to a boil and reduce the heat to a simmer. Cook until fork-tender, 8 to 12 minutes. Immediately transfer the potatoes, with a slotted spoon, to the ice bath. Drain well and pat dry. Cut in half lengthwise or, if large, into quarters. Immediately drizzle with vermouth, while still warm. Season with salt and pepper. Set aside.

5. Toss the lettuces with some of the anchovy-caper dressing and place on a large serving platter. Toss the potatoes, haricots verts, and cherry tomatoes separately with dressing and arrange over the lettuces. Add the tuna and olives. Arrange the eggs on the salad, season with salt and pepper, and serve.

Kale Caesar Salad

In the past few years, this has become a very, very popular salad, served in some fine restaurants as well as in many homes. I grow a lot of kale: I pick the Tuscan variety when it's young (removing any tough or large ribs) and chiffonade it—meaning to cut it into the thinnest crosswise strips—for this salad. The result is tender, tasty, and very palatable. The Caesar dressing is made the traditional way in a bowl, smashing the garlic and anchovy and salt—you can use a muddler, wooden pestle, or even the back of a spoon. Whisk in the lemon juice, Dijon mustard, and egg yolk, then thin out the dressing with olive oil before adding generous amounts of finely grated Parmigiano. Serve immediately, as one should serve all salads once dressed.

SERVES 6

2 garlic cloves

4 anchovy fillets, preferably salt-cured, rinsed if salted; or 2 teaspoons anchovy paste

Heaping ¼ teaspoon kosher salt

Pinch of freshly ground pepper

Juice from ½ lemon (about 2 tablespoons)

½ teaspoon Dijon mustard

1 large egg yolk

½ cup extra-virgin olive oil

2 ounces Parmigiano-Reggiano, finely grated (1 cup)

3 heads Tuscan kale, washed, dried, stems removed, leaves cut into ¼-inch strips

Brioche Croutons (recipe follows)

1. Place the garlic, anchovy fillets, salt, and pepper in a large wooden salad bowl. Using a muddler or two dinner forks, mash them to form a paste. Using one fork, whisk in the lemon juice, mustard, and egg yolk. While whisking, drizzle in the oil and continue to whisk until emulsified. Whisk in ½ cup of the grated cheese.

2. Add the kale, some croutons, and the remaining ½ cup cheese to the bowl. Toss well and serve.

Brioche Croutons
MAKES ABOUT 4 CUPS

Preheat the oven to 350°F. Line a rimmed baking sheet with parchment. Remove the crusts of ½ (1 pound) loaf **brioche bread** and cut into ¼-inch cubes. Toss the bread with 3 tablespoons extra-virgin **olive oil**, 1 melted tablespoon **butter**, 1 teaspoon kosher **salt**, and ½ teaspoon freshly ground **pepper**. Bake in a single layer until the croutons are toasted and crisp, 12 to 15 minutes, tossing halfway through.

Frisée Salad with Lardons & Poached Egg

1   **medium shallot, finely chopped**

4½   **teaspoons sherry vinegar**

1   **teaspoon Dijon mustard**

¼   **cup extra-virgin olive oil**

     Kosher salt and freshly ground pepper

8   **ounces thick-cut bacon, cut into ½-inch pieces**

4   **large eggs**

3   **heads of frisée, inner white part only, washed well and spun dry, torn into bite-size pieces**

1   **small bunch watercress, washed well and spun dry**

When I went to Paris for the first time to model, I stayed at the Hôtel Scandinavia on the rue de Tournon. I was so excited to have a croissant every morning with confiture d'abricots and café au lait. The small and cozy bistros in the neighborhood were known for their authentic and delicious food. One in particular served a most delightful salade frisée. I can still taste the lardons and the perfect vinaigrette that dressed the crisp greens. The farm-fresh egg atop everything was also poached to perfection, so when my fork broke through the white, a deep golden-yellow yolk oozed out. New York at that time was just getting familiar with real French cuisine, and Julia Child was sharing her recipes and those of her French friends with all of us who wanted to experiment with French cooking at home. Simple dishes, like this salad, could be mastered, and once the proper ingredients were located, like the French bacon from which to slice and sauté the lardons, the dish could emulate very nicely what I had experienced in Paris.

SERVES 4

1. In a salad bowl, combine the shallot, vinegar, and mustard; whisk to combine. Slowly whisk in the oil until well combined; season the vinaigrette with salt and pepper. Set aside.

2. Cook the bacon, stirring occasionally, in a medium skillet over medium-high heat until golden brown and the fat has rendered, 6 to 8 minutes. Transfer the bacon to a plate lined with a paper towel to drain.

3. Fill a large, deep skillet two-thirds full of water and bring to a boil. Reduce to a simmer.

4. Break an egg into a small bowl; holding the bowl just over the simmering water, gently slide the egg into the water. Repeat with the remaining eggs. Poach 1 to 2 minutes (longer for firm yolks). Use a slotted spoon to remove the poached eggs, and place on a paper towel to drain.

5. Add the frisée, watercress, and bacon to the salad bowl, and toss gently with the vinaigrette to combine. Divide evenly among 4 serving plates. Top each salad with one poached egg. (I love to slice the egg to show the yolk.) Season with salt and pepper. Serve immediately.

Cocktails

Martha-tinis

Crushed ice, for
cocktail shaker

16 ounces (2 cups) vodka,
such as Żubrówka Bison
Grass

3 ounces (about ⅓ cup) dry
vermouth, such as Dolin

Wide strips of lemon zest
or orange wedges, for
serving

Cocktail picks,
such as bamboo knot
picks, for serving

I have a couple of friends who turned me on to the ladylike habit of having one very good martini before dinner. The objective? If you add more ice as you sip the icy cold vodka, subtly flavored with a twist of lemon or orange, there is no need whatsoever for more than one drink. The one delicious martini can last throughout the entire dinner! Recently, I discovered an interesting Polish vodka called Żubrówka, which I use with Dolin vermouth in the Martha-tinis we serve at The Bedford by Martha Stewart, my restaurant in Las Vegas. Carefully measured, the spirits are shaken vigorously with crushed ice. When poured, shards of ice float atop the drink, adding a chill that is enticing. If you have individual martini shakers for your guests, you can pour a little heavier and leave the shaker alongside each guest's plate for an additional sip or two. A lemon twist is a beautiful and flavorful garnish. Use a bamboo or silver pick to loosely fold the peel and float it in the drink. Or you could serve the cocktail with a colorful and fragrant orange wedge.

MAKES 4 DRINKS

1. Fill a large shaker with crushed ice, the vodka, and the vermouth. Shake the cocktails until extra cold, for 40 to 60 shakes. Strain into chilled martini glasses (there should be shards of ice in the drinks).

2. Express a strip of lemon zest over the top of a cocktail, then skewer it on a cocktail pick, place in the drink, and serve. Repeat for each cocktail.

RAISE A GLASS

Call it the fin de siècle or the beginning of the twenty-first century, the millennium was celebrated everywhere with dinners and parties and news events. When this photo was taken for *Martha Stewart Living,* we were preparing for a special celebratory January 2000 issue. One of our core content areas at the magazine was entertaining, and we devoted many pages to new recipes, menus, and traditional displays for every holiday. To this day, many of those issues are treasured by our readers, including by me! I love dressing up and entertaining with flair, great food, a beautiful table, and delicious drinks. I entertain several times a month, sometimes simply for breakfast or lunch, other times with a full table of eighteen for dinner. I have used the recipes in this book many times to treat my friends and family to delicious meals and drinks. I love to concoct cocktails, mocktails, punches, and nogs. My eggnog from *Entertaining* has been made by so many people that it has become a staple for Christmas parties. The drinks in this section are absolutely wonderful—only fresh juices, the best spirits, and correct glassware are used. Serve these to your friends and you will become everyone's favorite bartender!

Photo by Todd Eberle, 1999

Frozen Pomegranate Martha-ritas

Turbinado sugar or
pink sea salt, for the rims
of glasses

18 ounces (2¼ cups)
fresh lime juice (about
18 limes)

16 ounces (2 cups) blanco
tequila, such as Casa
Dragones, chilled

 4 ounces (½ cup) triple sec,
such as Stirrings or
Cointreau

 4 ounces (½ cup)
pomegranate
concentrate

Ice, for blender

Many years ago, I met a fascinating couple from Philadelphia called the Resnicks. Lynda and her husband, Stewart, were serious entrepreneurs; they owned, at the time, The Franklin Mint, as well as other venturesome and successful companies. (I even made some designs for The Franklin Mint!) When the Resnicks moved to California, they started buying orange and other citrus, almond, and pomegranate orchards all over the state, smartly realizing the importance of the fruit and juice businesses that were about to burgeon. They understood that pomegranates in particular had unique and healthful qualities. My favorite of their products is POM Wonderful pomegranate juice concentrate, which is the base for my signature frozen cocktail. If you cannot locate it, you can use frozen pomegranate syrup. Serve Martha-ritas in large, beautiful goblets, as that is how they look and taste best!

MAKES 4 TO 6 DRINKS

1. Spread turbinado sugar on a small plate. Pour about 2 ounces (¼ cup) lime juice in a bowl. Dip the rims of the goblets in the lime juice then the sugar to create sugared rims.

2. Add the remaining 16 ounces (2 cups) lime juice, the tequila, triple sec, and pomegranate concentrate to a blender. Add ice. Blend on high until you no longer hear any ice crunching around and the drink is icy, frothy, and pinky red. Pour into the prepared glasses and serve.

Mary's Knees

Ice, for cocktail shaker and serving

4 ounces (½ cup) fresh orange juice (from 2 to 3 oranges)

2 ounces (¼ cup) vodka, such as Belvedere

1 ounce (2 tablespoons) Grand Marnier

1 ounce (2 tablespoons) fresh lemon juice (from 1 lemon)

1 ounce (2 tablespoons) fresh lime juice (from 1 lime)

Dried or fresh orange slices, for serving

This has been a favorite brunch cocktail since the 1980s, when I was catering a lot of brunch and luncheon parties. It was designed to be a citrus-juice alternative to the tomato-based Bloody Mary, which has certainly never fallen out of favor. What is absolutely essential in this drink is freshly squeezed orange, lemon, and lime juices. Vodka is the alcohol of choice, as is Grand Marnier. You can serve Mary's Knees with the fresh fruit slices you have on hand, but I also like the fun and modern touch of oven-dried, sugar-coated thin slices of seedless oranges, blood oranges, or even lemons.

MAKES 2 DRINKS

1. Fill a cocktail shaker with ice and pour in the orange juice, vodka, Grand Marnier, lemon juice, and lime juice. Shake the cocktail until extra cold, for 40 to 60 shakes. Strain over ice into 2 wine glasses.

2. Garnish with an orange slice and serve.

Mint Juleps

17 lemons

4 cups granulated sugar

Turbinado or granulated sugar, for rims of glasses

32 mint sprigs, plus more for serving

Ice cubes or crushed ice, for serving

24 ounces (3 cups) Kentucky bourbon, such as Woodford Reserve

I remember being invited to a fabulous homestead outside of Charleston to view the Kentucky Derby. The host was a single gentleman with a penchant for American history, antiques, and well-made cocktails. I wanted to surprise him with the best mint julep he had ever tasted. I tested and tweaked many recipes, and this is the superior one by far! I like to make a big batch for a crowd, so I start with seventeen lemons, preferably Meyer, to make the sweet, sugary syrup that forms the base of the drink. The syrup is best when prepared the day before serving and chilled with all the lemon peels. Of course, the most important ingredient other than the lemon syrup is the bourbon, and I love Woodford Reserve. Rimming the silver cups with raw sugar is a tasty added touch, as is the candied lemon peel garnish. A big sprig of fresh mint is essential.

MAKES 16 DRINKS

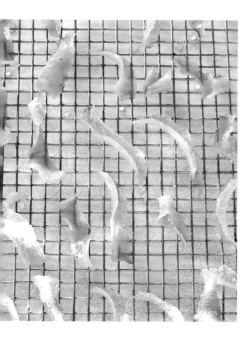

1. Line a baking sheet with parchment and a wire rack; set aside.

2. Using a vegetable peeler, remove the zest in wide strips from 4 lemons (reserve the zested lemons). Combine 1 cup sugar and 1 cup water in a small saucepan over medium-high heat. Bring to a simmer, stirring to dissolve the sugar. Add the lemon zest and simmer until translucent, about 1 hour. Let the zest cool in the liquid. Transfer the candied lemon peels to the wire rack to dry.

3. Squeeze all the lemons, reserving the rinds and juice separately. In a large saucepan over medium-high heat, combine the remaining 3 cups sugar with 3 cups of water, stirring until dissolved. Add the lemon rinds and cook over medium heat until the liquid becomes syrupy, about 15 minutes. Remove the pot from the heat and let stand until room temperature. Remove and discard the lemon rinds.

4. Spread the turbinado sugar on a small plate. Pour about ¼ cup lemon juice into a bowl. Dip the rims of 16 mint-julep cups or tall glasses in lemon juice then turbinado sugar to create sugared rims.

5. Use a muddler or a wooden spoon to crush a few mint leaves in the bottom of each prepared cup. Fill the cups with ice. Add about ¼ cup lemon juice and ½ cup lemon rind syrup to each cup. Top each with 1½ ounces bourbon. Garnish with a sprig of mint and a candied lemon peel.

White Cosmos

MAKES 2 DRINKS

Fill a cocktail shaker with **ice** and pour in 8 ounces (1 cup) **white cranberry juice**, 4 ounces (½ cup) **vodka**, such as Belvedere, and 2 ounces (¼ cup) **Cointreau**. Shake until extra cold, for 40 to 60 shakes. Strain into 2 chilled glasses, add **ice** (an ice sphere is a nice touch), and serve.

Cider-Bourbon Cocktails

MAKES 10 TO 12 DRINKS

Spread **turbinado sugar** on a small plate. Pour 2 ounces (¼ cup) **lemon juice** in a small bowl. Dip the rims of old-fashioned glasses first into the lemon juice and then into the sugar to create sugared rims. Into a large pitcher, add 36 ounces (4½ cups) **apple cider**, 12 ounces (1½ cups) **bourbon**, and 4 ounces (½ cup) fresh **lemon juice** (from 3 lemons). Stir together to combine. Pour a cocktail over an ice sphere in each glass and garnish with an **apple** slice.

Meyer Lemon Drop Cocktails

MAKES 2 DRINKS

Put 2 ounces (¼ cup) fresh **Meyer lemon juice** (from 2 lemons) and **sugar** in separate shallow bowls. Dip the rims of 2 coupe glasses first in the lemon juice then in the sugar. Fill a cocktail shaker with **ice** and pour in 4 ounces (½ cup) **vodka**, such as Belvedere, 1 ounce (2 tablespoons) **Cointreau**, 2 ounces (¼ cup) **Meyer lemon juice**, and 1 tablespoon **Meyer lemon simple syrup**. Shake until extra cold, for 40 to 60 shakes. Strain the cocktail into the prepared coupe glasses (there should be shards of ice in the drinks). Express a strip of lemon zest over the top of each cocktail, then skewer it on a cocktail pick, place in the drink, and serve.

Meyer Lemon Simple Syrup

MAKES ABOUT ½ CUP

Heat ½ cup **sugar** and 6 strips **Meyer lemon zest** (from 1 lemon) with ½ cup **water** in a small saucepan, stirring, until the sugar dissolves (don't bring to a boil). Remove from the heat and let the syrup cool. (Store simple syrup in an airtight glass container in the refrigerator up to 3 weeks.)

MARTHA'S NOTE

This is hardly a cocktail but rather more of an after-dinner sipping drink. I like to pour Cointreau over ice in a small, beautiful glass and sip it very slowly, letting my lips get coated with the sugar of the liqueur. I love to kiss someone after sipping Cointreau this way—it's a very sweet and tasty kiss!

Caipirinhas

Turbinado sugar, for
the rims of the glasses

2 ounces (¼ cup) fresh
lime juice (2 limes), plus
2 limes, quartered

¼ cup granulated sugar

4 ounces (½ cup) cachaça

Crushed ice, for serving

Several of my staff at the farm and, before that, at Turkey Hill, my home in Westport, Connecticut, came from Brazil. They have taught me recipes, dances, and gardening techniques over the years. My favorite Brazilian recipes? Salpicão (chicken salad), feijoada (black bean stew), and the national Brazilian drink, caipirinha, using the sugarcane liquor known as cachaça. This is my favorite summertime party drink, and I serve it in sugar-rimmed glasses at my gatherings in Maine. The ingredients are simple—fresh lime, sugar, crushed ice, and cachaça—and they can be either stirred or shaken. I try to have a large tray of these drinks ready for when guests arrive, and the cocktails always disappear quickly.

MAKES 2 DRINKS

MARTHA'S NOTE

I often serve a passion-fruit caipirinha as well—it's delicious! Follow the recipe here and simply add 1 tablespoon **passion-fruit puree** per glass when adding the cachaça in step 2.

1. Spread turbinado sugar on a small plate. Pour 2 ounces (¼ cup) lime juice into a bowl. Dip the rims of the glasses in the lime juice then the sugar to create sugared rims.

2. Place 4 lime quarters and 2 tablespoons sugar in each glass. Muddle well. Top each with 2 ounces cachaça and crushed ice. Stir together to combine.

Espresso Martinis

Ice, for cocktail shaker

2 ounces (¼ cup) vodka, such as Belvedere or Żubrówka Bison Grass

1 ounce (2 tablespoons) coffee liqueur, such as Kahlúa or Tia Maria

1 double-shot of espresso

Every so often, a new cocktail appears on the menus of all the fancy restaurants. I remember when the white cosmo was all the rage and when the caipirinha became so very popular, both of which I still adore. At present, it seems that the espresso martini has assumed the distinctive status. I personally do not drink espresso, but when mixed with vodka and Kahlúa or Tia Maria, that very strong essence of coffee assumes a sexiness and appeal I never would have expected. I can actually drink one of these cocktails happily in lieu of a dessert offering—it's very, very good with a small scoop of vanilla ice cream.

MAKES 2 DRINKS

1. Fill a shaker with ice and pour in the vodka, coffee liqueur, and espresso. Shake vigorously until the outside of the shaker is frosty, at least 40 to 60 shakes.

2. Strain into two glasses and serve immediately.

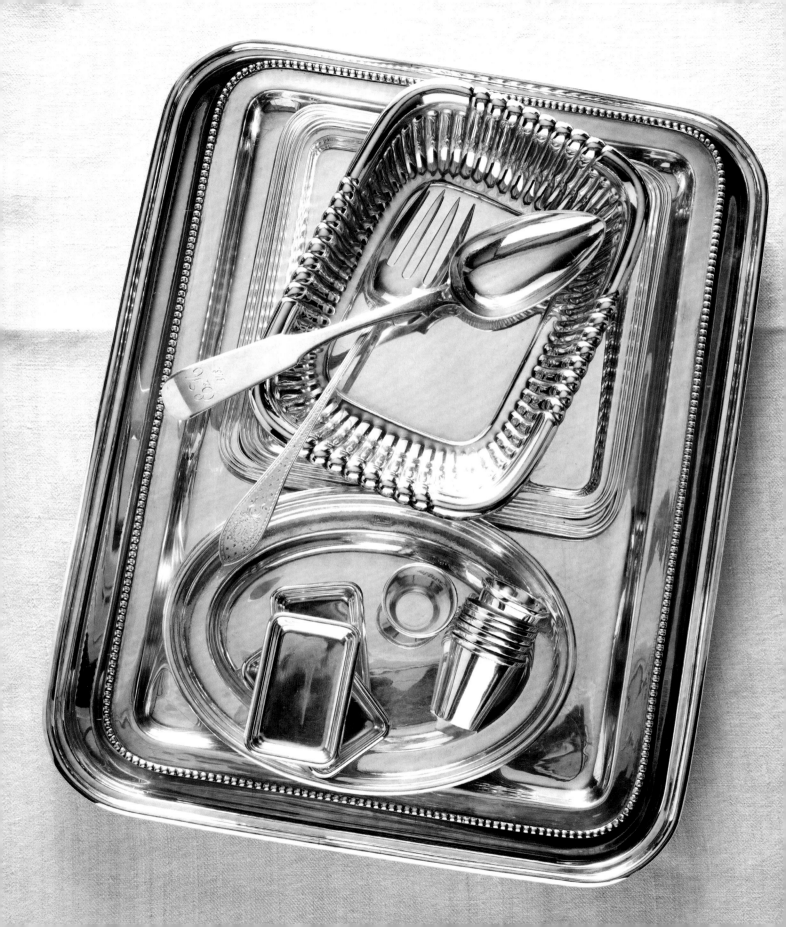

Hors d'Oeuvres

Gougères

1 stick (½ cup) unsalted butter

½ teaspoon kosher salt

1 cup unbleached all-purpose flour

8 large eggs, plus 1 white for egg wash

2½ ounces Comté cheese, finely grated (¾ cup)

2½ ounces Gruyère cheese, finely grated (¾ cup)

1 ounce Parmigiano-Reggiano, finely grated (½ cup)

Gougères are one of my very favorite light hors d'oeuvres to serve before a dinner or at a cocktail party. I have been making pâte à choux puffs with cheese for many years but only recently discovered that the simple addition of more eggs yields even airier and more delectable results. Past recipes I've followed have called for four eggs to one cup of flour. I now use up to eight eggs for lighter puffs with larger open centers. I also sprinkle the finely grated cheeses atop each puff after piping, rather than incorporating the cheeses into the dough. You can easily see the voluptuous puffs in the photograph. They are beautiful, not filling, and eminently delicious.

MAKES ABOUT 60 GOUGÈRES

1. Preheat the oven to 375°F. Line three rimmed baking sheets with parchment.

2. In a small saucepan, bring 1 cup water, the butter, and salt to a boil. Remove from the heat. With a wooden spoon, stir in the flour until the mixture pulls aways from the sides of the pan, 2 to 4 minutes. Let it cool for 2 minutes.

3. Add the eggs, one at a time, mixing after each addition and until the batter comes together. Transfer the batter to a pastry bag fitted with a ½-inch plain tip (such as Ateco #806). Pipe the batter onto the prepared sheets into desired mounds, about 1 inch apart.

4. Mix the three grated cheeses in a small bowl. Brush the tops of the puffs with the egg white and then sprinkle them with grated cheese. Bake one sheet at a time for 10 minutes. Reduce the oven temperature to 350°F and bake until the puffs are golden brown and feel light and hollow inside, 20 to 30 minutes more. Serve immediately.

Crepes with Crème Fraîche & Caviar

Here, the ultimate buckwheat crepes on which to add generous amounts of crème fraîche and a best-quality caviar. Generally, the crepes that accompany these toppings are one-bite size. These larger ones were inspired by an Easter brunch I attended in Moscow years ago during my first visit there. Piles of crepes were brought to the table, accompanied by giant bowls of beluga caviar, crème fraîche, and lovely spoons with which to dollop! Try these—they do not disappoint.

MAKES ABOUT 36 CREPES

3½ cups whole milk

8 large eggs

6 tablespoons unsalted butter, melted and cooled; plus 4 tablespoons, softened, for cooking crepes

1 cup buckwheat flour

1 cup unbleached all-purpose flour

1½ teaspoons kosher salt

Crème fraîche, for serving

Caviar, such as Black Diamond, for serving

1. Combine the milk, eggs, melted butter, both flours, and salt in a blender. Puree until smooth, about 1 minute. Transfer to a bowl, cover, and refrigerate until cold, for at least 2 hours and up to 1 day.

2. Whisk the batter until smooth. Melt ½ teaspoon butter in an 8-inch nonstick skillet or crepe pan over medium heat. Tilt the skillet at a 45-degree angle, pour in a scant 3 tablespoons (about 1½ ounces), and immediately swirl and shake the skillet in a circular motion to evenly distribute the batter in a very thin film across the bottom. Cook until the edges of the crepe turn golden, about 45 seconds. Carefully flip the crepe and cook just until set, about 30 seconds.

3. Transfer to a paper-towel-lined plate. Melt another ½ teaspoon butter and continue cooking the remaining crepes in the same manner, whisking the batter between crepes and stacking cooked crepes on top of one another. Let the crepes cool completely, about 30 minutes, before serving with crème fraîche and caviar.

Potato Pancakes

4 large baking potatoes, such as Idaho or russet, peeled

Ice water, for grated potatoes

1 small yellow onion

2 large eggs, lightly beaten

¼ cup lager

3 tablespoons unbleached all-purpose flour

Kosher salt and freshly ground pepper

Vegetable oil, such as safflower or rice bran oil, for frying

Sour cream, for serving

Pink Applesauce (page 270), for serving

Big Martha taught me the basic recipe for these crispy, crunchy potato pancakes. I make them often—sometimes to serve as a vegetable course for a holiday dinner, but mostly as hors d'oeuvres. Use baking potatoes, which are starchy and crisp up nicely: Peel them and then grate them by hand on a box grater. Soak the grated potatoes in ice water until just before using, to prevent them from oxidizing. Drain them well and reserve the starchy residue in the bottom of the bowl, stirring it into the mix to help bind the potato pancakes. I also add beer, which I find provides some lightness and crispness. I like to top the potato pancakes with sour cream and pink applesauce, crème fraîche and caviar, or sour cream and smoked salmon. Any way you choose, they are perfect.

SERVES 6 (MAKES ABOUT TWENTY 3-INCH PANCAKES)

1. Using smooth strokes, grate the potatoes in long shreds across the large holes of a grater into a large bowl of ice water. Set a sieve or colander over a large bowl and drain the potatoes, squeezing out excess liquid. Reserve the liquid. Set the liquid aside until the starch sinks to the bottom of the bowl, about 10 minutes. Carefully pour the liquid from the bowl and discard, reserving the milky residue (potato starch). Transfer the potatoes to the bowl with the potato starch.

2. Meanwhile, grate the onion. Add the grated onion to the grated potatoes. Stir in the eggs, lager, flour, 1½ teaspoons salt, and ½ teaspoon pepper.

3. Preheat the oven to 200°F. Line a baking sheet with paper towels; set aside. In a heavy skillet, heat a scant ½ inch oil. Spoon 2 tablespoons to ¼ cup potato mixture per pancake into the skillet. (Make a few at a time, being careful that they don't run into one another.)

4. Fry the pancakes, flipping once, until golden brown on both sides, about 5 minutes total. Add more oil as needed between batches. Transfer to the prepared baking sheet to drain and keep warm in the oven while frying the rest. Serve warm with sour cream and applesauce.

Deviled Eggs

12 Silkie farm eggs or medium-size eggs, at room temperature

¼ cup mayonnaise, plus more if needed

1 to 2 teaspoons Dijon mustard

Kosher salt and freshly ground pepper

2 tablespoons unsalted butter, melted

Serving suggestions: dill or tarragon sprigs, snipped chives, sweet paprika, and chopped dried chiles

So many eateries offer a version of this popular dish. Elegant, uncracked halves of egg whites filled with a tasty, creamy egg yolk filling that's garnished with various colorful toppings. Deviled eggs are so much fun to make at home. The trick is to steam and peel the eggs correctly: Use older eggs, as they are easier to peel, and start peeling at the broad end of the egg, where the air pocket generally is. I like to use my farm eggs, particularly those from my Silkie hens, who lay small, beautiful eggs with a nice proportion of white to yolk. Don't use very large eggs, as they are really more than a mouthful.

MAKES 24 DEVILED EGGS

1. Prepare an ice bath in a large bowl. Fill a large pot with 2 inches of water, insert a steamer basket, and bring the water to a boil. Add the eggs, cover, and steam them: 6 minutes for Silkie eggs; 11 to 12 minutes for medium-size. Remove the eggs from the pot and transfer to the ice bath to stop the cooking. Transfer to a colander to drain.

2. Peel the eggs and cut in half lengthwise (for cleanest eggs, wipe the blade between cuts). Remove the yolks, keeping the whites intact.

3. In a bowl, mash the yolks with a fork, then transfer them to a coarse-mesh sieve. Using a flexible spatula, press the yolks through the sieve into a medium bowl. Stir in the mayonnaise, mustard, and salt and pepper to taste. Mix to combine. Stir in the butter until creamy and smooth (if not creamy enough, add more mayonnaise, 1 tablespoon at a time). Taste and adjust for seasoning.

4. Fill a pastry bag fitted with a large star (or other large) tip and fill each half egg. (This can be made ahead up to this point and refrigerated, covered, for up to 3 hours.) Top with desired garnishes and serve.

MARTHA'S NOTE

Slice a small piece off the bottom of each boiled egg half to keep eggs from toppling over—it's a good thing!

Oysters, Two Ways

FOR THE BÉCHAMEL

- 2 tablespoons unsalted butter
- 5 teaspoons unbleached all-purpose flour
- ½ cup heavy cream
- ½ cup whole milk
- ½ teaspoon kosher salt

FOR THE FILLING

- 1 teaspoon extra-virgin olive oil
- 3½ cups fresh baby or flat-leaf spinach, stemmed, washed, and drained
- 1 cup watercress leaves
- 1 tablespoon unsalted butter
- ½ small yellow onion, diced
- Kosher salt and freshly ground pepper
- 6 flat-leaf parsley sprigs, finely chopped
- 3 tarragon sprigs, finely chopped
- 1 tablespoon Pernod
- ½ ounce Parmigiano-Reggiano, finely grated (⅓ cup)
- ¼ cup heavy cream

FOR THE OYSTERS AND TOPPING

- ¼ cup panko breadcrumbs
- 3 flat-leaf parsley sprigs, finely chopped
- 24 East Coast oysters, Blue Point preferred, shucked and shells cleaned
- Lemon wedges, for serving

At my home on Mount Desert Island, Maine, plump, briny oysters are plentiful. We often serve them as a luncheon dish, as a first course for dinner, or with cocktails. When my dear friend and Maine neighbor, David Rockefeller, Sr.—or "Mister," as we all called him—would come to dine, we especially loved making oysters Rockefeller. My version is rich, the béchamel topping filled with watercress as well as traditional spinach, and flavored with tarragon and Pernod. And for a spicier alternative, we like to serve the oysters casino-style. I think you will love these recipes; "Mister" loved both versions!

EACH RECIPE MAKES 24 OYSTERS AND SERVES 8

The Oyster Rockefeller

1. Make the béchamel: In a medium saucepan, melt the butter over low heat. Add the flour and cook, stirring frequently, until the mixture is pale golden, 2 to 3 minutes.

2. Add the cream and milk and whisk until smooth. Cook the mixture, stirring constantly on low heat until thickened, 4 to 5 minutes. Season with salt. Set aside to cool.

3. Make the filling: In a sauté pan, heat the oil. Sauté the spinach until just wilted. Transfer to a colander and squeeze the spinach to remove as much liquid as possible. Using a sharp knife, finely chop the spinach. Add the watercress to the same pan and repeat the process.

4. In the same pan, melt the butter. Add the onion and cook until lightly browned, 6 to 8 minutes. Season with salt and pepper. Set aside to cool.

5. Preheat the oven to 450°F. In a bowl, combine the chopped spinach, watercress, parsley, and tarragon. Add the béchamel, Pernod, cheese, cooked onion, and cream. Season with salt and pepper and set aside.

6. Make the topping: In a small bowl, mix together the panko and parsley.

7. Place a piece of loosely crumpled foil on a rimmed baking sheet to keep the oysters from falling over. Divide the topping mixture evenly among the oysters, placing each on the foil as you work. Sprinkle with the parsley-panko breadcrumbs.

8. Bake for 8 minutes. Turn the oven to broil and broil until the topping is golden brown, 3 to 4 minutes.

continued

THE OYSTER
ROCKEFELLER

OYSTERS
CASINO

4   slices bacon, chopped

1   stick (½ cup) unsalted butter

½   cup minced shallots

¼   cup finely chopped red bell pepper

¼   cup finely chopped celery

1   tablespoon fresh lemon juice, plus lemon wedges for serving

¼   teaspoon Worcestershire sauce

    Large pinch of cayenne pepper

24 (3- to 4-inch-long) East Coast oysters, Blue Point preferred, shucked and shells cleaned

Oysters Casino

1. Preheat the oven to 400°F. In a small skillet, cook the bacon until almost crisp, 6 to 8 minutes. (The bacon will continue to cook in the oven.) Using a slotted spoon, transfer the bacon to a paper towel–lined plate and set aside.

2. Place the butter, shallots, bell pepper, celery, lemon juice, Worcestershire sauce, and cayenne in a food processor, and mix until well combined, about 20 seconds.

3. Place a piece of loosely crumpled foil on a rimmed baking sheet to keep the oysters from falling over. Place 1 tablespoon of the butter mixture on each oyster and top each with bacon. Place on the foil–lined sheet. Bake the oysters until bubbly, about 12 minutes. Do not overcook. Serve immediately with lemon wedges.

SKYLANDS

I have owned my beautiful Edsel Ford home on Mount Desert Island
for more than twenty-five years. The large stone terrace, facing
the ocean and the Maine islands east of Mount Desert, is a perfect place
to entertain. As it is very suited to large outdoor and indoor
gatherings, we often use Skylands for philanthropic fundraisers for
garden, nature, and environmental causes. In Maine, there is a
tremendous amount of sustainable and careful sea-focused aquaculture
going on—oysters are being raised very successfully all along the
Eastern Seaboard, and scallops are being grown in the open ocean
on strings suspended right down to the ocean depths. Mussels are
being farmed, and so are clams. Creating viable habitats and rebuilding
stocks of species that are in danger of being overharvested is key
to being environmentally responsible.

Photo by Frédéric Lagrange, 2012

Cheese Straps

1 teaspoon paprika
or cayenne pepper

2 ounces Parmigiano-
Reggiano or Gruyère
cheese, finely grated
(about 1 cup)

1 pound homemade Puff
Pastry (page 290; about
⅓ of recipe) or store-
bought puff pastry (such
as Lecoq Cuisine)

¼ cup toasted poppy seeds
(optional)

When Julia Child and Simone Beck's famous sequel, *Mastering the Art of French Cooking, Volume Two,* was published in 1970, I was elated! Finally, a cookbook with recipes for the most illustrious of French pastries and breads, including baguettes, brioche, and pâte feuilletée—also known as puff pastry. I immediately started baking them all from scratch, and I was especially enamored with puff pastry, which was considered to be one of the most challenging and also one of the most versatile pastries in the world. The delicate dough, layered with butter, is fun to make, lovely to roll, and surprisingly delightful to shape into various forms, including palmiers, Napoleons, tart shells, and cheese straws. I adore cheese straws as well as poppy seed straws. Enjoy!

MAKES 3 DOZEN

1. In a medium bowl, mix the paprika with the cheese. Sprinkle the mixture on a work surface. Roll the puff pastry on the cheese-coated surface, to a rectangle approximately 10 inches by 13 inches, pressing the dough into the cheese to adhere. For the poppy seed straws, sprinkle the top of the dough with the poppy seeds; press the dough with your rolling pin to adhere.

2. Trim the sides with a pastry wheel cutter. (You will have a rectangle that is roughly 9 by 12 inches.) Cut the puff pastry into ¾-inch strips and twist from one end to the other. Arrange the strips, 1½ inches apart, on a baking sheet. Refrigerate the straws on the baking sheet until very firm, about 45 minutes.

3. Preheat the oven to 375°F. Bake the straws in the center of the oven until golden brown and puffed, 20 to 25 minutes. Transfer the cheese straws, and poppy seed straws if making, to a wire rack to cool. Repeat with the remaining puff pastry.

Crab Cakes

FOR THE TARTAR SAUCE

- 1 cup mayonnaise
- ⅓ cup finely chopped cornichons
- ¼ cup drained chopped capers
- 1 tablespoon finely chopped preserved lemon
- ½ teaspoon finely grated lemon zest
- Kosher salt and freshly ground pepper

FOR THE CRAB CAKES

- 1 pound crabmeat, such as peekytoe
- 1½ cups fresh brioche breadcrumbs ground (from ¼ loaf)
- ⅔ cup diced roasted yellow bell pepper
- ¼ cup chopped cilantro
- Kosher salt and freshly ground pepper
- ½ cup mayonnaise
- ½ teaspoon finely grated lemon zest, plus ¼ cup fresh lemon juice (from 2 lemons)
- 2 large eggs
- 1 cup unbleached all-purpose flour
- 1 cup panko breadcrumbs
- Vegetable oil, for cooking
- Celeriac Slaw (recipe follows), for serving
- Chive blossoms or watercress, for serving

Ever since I went crabbing for blue crabs with my father, Edward Kostyra, in the Shrewsbury River in New Jersey, I have loved the taste of hard-shell crabs. I love the art of catching them on strings dropped off the side of a skiff bobbing in the fresh ocean water. I love the process of quickly steaming them, cooling them, and removing the sweet, flaky meat. And because I now have a house in Maine, I love having access to freshly picked peekytoe crabmeat, as well. I use either type in my crab cakes, which we serve as finger-food hors d'oeuvres, or as a main course for lunch or dinner. I encourage you to prepare these cakes with care, handling the lumps of crab gently so as not to mush them up. The mayonnaise and eggs act as binders, preventing the cakes from falling apart. Chilling the patties well, before cooking them to perfection in hot vegetable oil (I prefer rice bran oil), will also help them retain their shape.

MAKES ABOUT 12 CRAB CAKES

1. Make the tartar sauce: In a bowl, combine the mayonnaise, cornichons, capers, preserved lemon, and lemon zest. Season with salt and pepper.

2. Make the crab cakes: In a large bowl, combine the crabmeat, brioche breadcrumbs, roasted yellow pepper, and cilantro. Gently toss to combine. Season with salt and pepper.

3. In a small bowl, combine the mayonnaise, lemon zest, and lemon juice. Add the lemon-mayonnaise mixture to the crab mixture and gently combine by hand, ensuring not to break up any of the crab pieces.

4. Using a ¼ cup or 2-inch scoop, make 12 crab cakes. Place them on a parchment-lined baking sheet and chill in the refrigerator until firm, at least 1 hour.

continued

5. Preheat the oven to 450°F. Whisk the eggs in a bowl. Dredge the crab cakes in the flour, tapping off any excess. Dip in the eggs, allow excess to drip off, then coat with panko, patting to adhere.

6. Heat a thin layer of oil in a large skillet over medium–high. Cook the crab cakes until golden brown, 1 to 2 minutes per side. Transfer to a clean baking sheet lined with parchment and bake until cooked through, about 10 minutes. Serve topped with tartar sauce, with a side of celeriac slaw, and garnished with chive blossoms.

Celeriac Slaw
SERVES 12

Slice ½ peeled **celeriac**, 1 unpeeled green **apple**, and 2 **carrots** on a mandoline using the ⅛-inch julienne attachment. Place in a large bowl, add 1 tablespoon **lemon juice** and 1 teaspoon kosher **salt** and toss gently to combine. Let rest 20 minutes. Squeeze and discard the liquid. In a medium bowl, whisk together ¼ cup **lemon juice**, 2 tablespoons **Dijon mustard**, and 2 tablespoons **honey**. Season with a pinch of kosher **salt** and freshly ground **pepper**. Gradually whisk in 3 tablespoons extra-virgin **olive oil** and 1 tablespoon **sunflower oil** into the dressing until emulsified. Add 2 tablespoons dressing to the celeriac mixture and season with salt and pepper. Add more dressing, if needed.

Vegetable Flatbread

3 cups plus 1½ teaspoons unbleached all-purpose flour, plus more for dusting

1¼ teaspoons active dry yeast (from one ¼-ounce envelope)

Pinch of sugar

1¼ cups warm water (100°F to 110°F), plus more if necessary

¼ cup yellow cornmeal

¼ cup fresh rosemary needles

1 teaspoon kosher salt, plus more for sprinkling

1½ teaspoons freshly ground pepper, plus more for sprinkling

¼ cup extra-virgin olive oil, plus more for bowl

1 medium red onion, sliced very thinly

1 bunch fresh sage leaves

4 tomatillos, husked and thinly sliced

6 cherry tomatoes, thinly sliced

This is the most popular item in the breadbasket at The Bedford, my restaurant in Las Vegas. The so-thin-it's-nearly-translucent dough, studded with thinly sliced vegetables and herbs, looks almost like stained glass when baked. I was first served the crispy, easily snapped bread at a party in Connecticut catered by my friend Julie Williamson, fondly known as JuneBug. We adopted her version for the restaurant. Thanks, JuneBug—we love this beautiful and tasty bread!

MAKES 6 FLATBREADS

1. In the bowl of an electric mixer fitted with the whisk attachment, combine 1½ teaspoons flour, the yeast, and sugar. Stir in ¼ cup of the warm water and let stand until foamy, about 10 minutes.

2. In a large bowl, whisk together the remaining 3 cups of flour, the cornmeal, rosemary, salt, and pepper; add to the yeast mixture. Using the dough hook, mix on low speed while slowly adding the remaining 1 cup of warm water. Mix, adding more warm water if necessary, 1 tablespoon at a time, until the dough starts to pull away from the sides of the bowl and is smooth and elastic, 5 to 6 minutes. Turn out the dough onto a clean surface and knead 4 turns into a ball.

3. Place the dough in a lightly oiled large bowl and coat the dough with oil. Cover tightly with plastic wrap, and let the dough rise in a warm place until doubled in size, about 1 hour. Turn out onto a clean surface; divide into 6 even pieces, each about 4 inches long. Transfer the balls to a parchment-lined baking sheet and loosely cover them with plastic wrap.

4. Preheat the oven to 400°F. On a lightly floured surface, pat one of the balls into a 3-by-5-inch rectangle, then roll it out to a 5-by-17-inch rectangle; it should be very thin. Place on the diagonal on an ungreased baking sheet. Brush the surface of the dough with oil; arrange the onion slices, sage leaves, tomatillo slices, and tomato slices atop the flatbreads, dividing evenly. Sprinkle with salt and pepper. Brush again lightly with oil.

5. Bake until the flatbread turns golden brown, 12 to 14 minutes. Transfer the flatbread to a wire rack to cool. Repeat with the remaining dough: roll out, top, and bake. (Store in an airtight container for up to 1 week.)

Buckwheat Blini
with Caviar

1 (¼-ounce) envelope
active dry yeast
(2¼ teaspoons)

1½ cups warm water
(100°F to 110°F)

1½ cups unbleached
all-purpose flour

1½ cups buckwheat flour

1½ cups warm milk (100°F
to 110°F)

3 large eggs, separated

4 tablespoons unsalted
butter, melted,
plus more, softened,
for skillet

1 teaspoon sugar

Pinch of kosher salt

Sour cream, for serving

Caviar, such as roe,
for serving

Dill sprigs, for serving

When I ran a catering business, The Uncatered Affair, these silver-dollar blini were a mainstay of the appetizer list I offered to clients, and they remain one of my favorites today. Topped with red or black caviar; a rosette of smoked salmon; or a large segment of smoked trout, these small, light pancakes are sinfully delicious. They can be made ahead and frozen, and they reheat nicely well wrapped in parchment and foil. The batter is a yeast-risen dough and uses buckwheat flour, but you can use all white flour if you choose. I like to make the batter several hours before cooking the blini, which I do on a large, buttered flat skillet using a small ladle to keep the blini all the same size. Be sure the blini are cooked well on one side before flipping to cook the second side.

MAKES 75 COCKTAIL-SIZE BLINI

1. Combine the yeast and warm water in a medium bowl. Let stand until foamy, about 10 minutes.

2. Slowly stir the all-purpose flour into the yeast mixture. Cover and let the batter rise for 1 hour.

3. Combine the buckwheat flour, milk, egg yolks, butter, sugar, and salt with the batter. Stir well to blend all the ingredients. Cover and let rise for 1 hour.

4. Just before cooking, beat the egg whites until stiff and fold them into the batter.

5. Heat a heavy skillet or griddle over medium-high. Brush with butter. Working in batches, add 1 tablespoon of the batter for each blini and cook until lightly browned, about 2 minutes per side. Transfer the blini to a platter that has been heated to keep them warm.

6. To serve, put a dollop of sour cream, a spoonful of caviar, and a sprig of dill on the center of each blini.

Scallops Crudo

1 small shallot, minced

¼ cup seasoned rice vinegar

1 dozen sea scallops

Grated zest and juice of 1 lime

Grated zest of ½ orange

Grated zest of 1 lemon

½ tablespoon finely grated ginger

1 small jalapeño chile, seeded and finely minced

Cilantro sprigs, for serving

Chervil sprigs, for serving

In 1998, believe it or not, I donned a dry suit in January and dove in the Atlantic Ocean off the coast of Mount Desert Island to harvest sea scallops. I thought at the time, What an odd occupation, diving in 15-degree weather in the ocean for one of the sea's most delicious shellfish. The fishermen I was with set me straight: They pointed out that it was windy and cold, frigid, in fact, out of the water and a quiet, calm 38 degrees under the water. "Which do you prefer?" they asked me, as if I had a choice. The scallops we harvested that day were sweet, large, pinkish in color, and amazingly delicious. I was already an aficionado of raw fish and shellfish, and I ate a piece of scallop as it was served to me on the point of a knife, unadorned with anything. It was incredible. Now there are ambitious young fishermen who are learning to farm scallops on ropes suspended in the ocean depths in "scallop farms," just as the Japanese have done for many, many years. The scallops are just as tasty, just as beautiful, but are sustainably farmed in the clear, cold ocean. Below is a simple "crudo" recipe, where the scallops "cook" a bit in the mixture and the brininess of the flesh is enhanced by the vinegar and flavorings. Of course, the same scallops can be pan-seared, grilled, or cooked quickly in a paella. The ultimate point is to enjoy these magnificent beauties.

SERVES 2

1. In a small bowl, combine the shallot and vinegar.

2. Using a shellfish knife or a butter knife, shuck the scallops and remove the side muscles.

3. Using a sharp knife, cut each scallop crosswise into 3 even slices and arrange them on a plate. Cover and chill the scallops in the refrigerator.

4. Combine the shallot and vinegar mixture with the lime juice, zests, ginger, and jalapeño in a bowl. When ready to serve, transfer the scallops to 2 serving plates, drizzle with the dressing, and garnish with cilantro and chervil sprigs.

Laura's Baked Stuffed Clams

FOR THE CLAMS

2 tablespoons extra-virgin olive oil

1 small red onion, coarsely chopped

6 garlic cloves, crushed

1 cup dry white wine, such as Sauvignon Blanc

12 large or 15 small little-neck or cherrystone clams (each 2½ to 3 inches across), scrubbed

FOR THE FILLING

2 tablespoons extra-virgin olive oil

½ medium white onion, minced

1 garlic clove, minced

1 cup finely ground fresh breadcrumbs

½ cup almond flour (or finely ground blanched almonds)

½ cup finely chopped fresh flat-leaf parsley leaves (from 1 small bunch)

1 tablespoon finely chopped fresh dill

1 teaspoon finely chopped fresh thyme leaves

4 tablespoons unsalted butter, softened

Kosher salt and freshly ground pepper

Seaweed, for serving (optional)

Lemon wedges, for serving

My youngest sister, Laura, married Randy Plimpton on Cutchogue, Long Island, at the Plimpton family home, a beautiful nineteenth-century Tudor-style house on the white sandy beach along Long Island Sound. Laura's mother-in-law was famous for her baked stuffed clam recipe, which had been first published in the *Ladies' Village Improvement Society Cookbook*. Using large quahogs, dug right on their local beach, Laura was a masterful interpreter of the recipe. You be the witness.

MAKES 12 TO 15, DEPENDING ON SIZE OF CLAMS

1. Make the clams: Heat the oil in a large pot over medium-high. Add the onion and cook until softened but not browned, stirring occasionally, about 5 minutes. Add the garlic and sauté just until fragrant, about 1 minute.

2. Add the wine and bring to a simmer. Add the clams and stir to combine. Cover and steam until the clams open, 5 to 7 minutes. Remove from the heat. Use a slotted spoon to transfer the clams to a rimmed baking sheet to cool, discarding any that have not opened. Strain the clam broth through a fine-mesh sieve, and reserve the broth for making the filling; you'll need 4 to 6 tablespoons.

3. When the clams are cool enough to handle, remove all the meat and reserve. Remove half of each clam shell and discard. Clean the remaining halves and arrange on a rimmed baking sheet. Cut each clam into ½-inch pieces; return the pieces to the shell. (Clams can be prepared to this point up to 1 day ahead. Cover with plastic wrap and refrigerate.)

4. Make the filling: Preheat the oven to 350°F. Heat the oil in a sauté pan. Cook the onion and garlic until translucent, stirring frequently, about 5 minutes. Remove from the heat and let cool completely.

5. Stir together the onion mixture, breadcrumbs, almond flour, herbs, and butter in a bowl; season with salt and pepper. Stir in just enough clam broth to moisten the filling, 4 to 6 tablespoons.

6. Dividing evenly, press the breadcrumb filling into the clam shells, smoothing with the back of a spoon. Bake until the tops are golden, 25 to 30 minutes. Nestle the clams on the seaweed, if desired, and serve immediately with lemon wedges.

Glazed Country Ham with Angel Biscuits

1 (16-pound) country-cured ham

4 cups packed brown sugar

2 cups cognac

Angel Biscuits (recipe follows), for serving

Brooke's Mustard Dip (recipe follows), for serving

It is really hard to find a well-prepared country ham these days. I can still order one for holiday parties from the Loveless Cafe in Nashville, Tennessee, which is where I learned how to cook it carefully and well. The method of cooking in this recipe is unusual, but it eliminates the much more difficult process of boiling a country ham prior to skinning, scoring, and glazing. Try this—you will be surprised by how perfectly the technique works and you will certainly love the taste: The cognac brown-sugar glaze enhances each small, thin slice. I serve the country ham atop angel biscuits with a wonderful mustard dip.

SERVES ABOUT 20

Glazed Country Ham

1. Clean the ham with hot water and a stiff brush. Soak the ham for 24 hours in cold water to dilute the salt. Preheat the oven to 500°F. Wrap the ham well in parchment-lined foil and place in a roasting pan or on a rimmed baking sheet. Bake for 30 minutes. Turn off the oven and let the ham sit for 3 hours in the oven; do not open the door. After 3 hours, turn on the oven and bake at 500°F for 15 minutes. Turn off the oven but do not open the door. Leave the ham in the closed oven overnight.

2. Remove the ham from the oven and unwrap. Preheat the oven to 350°F. With a sharp knife, trim the rind and all but 1/8 to 1/4 inch of the fat from the ham; then score the fat in a tight diamond pattern.

3. In a medium bowl, combine the brown sugar and cognac to make the glaze. Spoon half the glaze over the ham and bake uncovered for 15 minutes. Spoon the remaining glaze over the ham and bake for another 20 minutes. Slice the ham into very thin slivers and serve it atop angel biscuits, with Brooke's mustard dip. The ham can be served hot or cold.

continued

2 (¼-ounce) envelopes of active dry yeast (4½ teaspoons total)

¼ cup warm water (100°F to 110°F)

5 cups unbleached all-purpose flour, plus more for dusting

2½ tablespoons sugar

1 tablespoon baking powder

1 teaspoon baking soda

1 teaspoon kosher salt

2 sticks (1 cup) unsalted butter, cut into small pieces; plus 1 stick (½ cup) unsalted butter, melted and cooled

2 cups buttermilk

Angel Biscuits

MAKES 32 (2¼-INCH) SQUARE BISCUITS

1. Preheat the oven to 450°F. Line a baking sheet with parchment and set aside.

2. Combine the yeast and warm water in a medium bowl. Let stand until foamy, about 10 minutes.

3. Whisk together the flour, sugar, baking powder, baking soda, and salt in a large bowl. Using a pastry blender or your fingers, cut in the butter pieces until the mixture resembles coarse meal. Stir in the yeast mixture and buttermilk. Turn out onto a floured board and knead the dough until it is smooth and no longer sticky.

4. Roll out the dough to a ½-inch thickness. Cut out shapes with a knife or biscuit cutter and set on the baking sheet. Brush the tops with the melted butter and bake until lightly golden, 10 to 12 minutes.

Brooke's Mustard Dip

MAKES ABOUT 1⅔ CUPS

Mix ¾ cup distilled **white vinegar**, ½ cup **dry mustard**, and ½ cup dry **white wine** or dry **vermouth** in a porcelain or stainless-steel bowl. Cover and let stand overnight. Beat 3 large **eggs** with ½ cup **sugar** and 1½ teaspoons kosher **salt** until very light and foamy, about 3 minutes. Add the mustard mixture and cook in a double boiler (or in a stainless-steel bowl over a pot of simmering water) until thick, approximately 1 hour, whisking occasionally. Let cool and refrigerate until ready to use.

Dinner

Tomato Tart

1 head of garlic, top third sliced off

¼ cup extra-virgin olive oil

Unbleached all-purpose flour, for dusting

1 disk (½ recipe) Pâte Brisée (page 288), chilled

3 ounces Italian fontina cheese, grated (about 1 cup)

1½ pounds firm but ripe tomatoes (4 medium), cored and sliced ¼ inch thick

Kosher salt and freshly ground pepper

Handful of cherry tomatoes, halved (optional)

Thyme sprigs, for serving

John Barricelli, owner of the SoNo Baking Company in Connecticut, taught me a version of this tomato tart when we were producing *The Martha Stewart Show* in Westport. He had learned his recipe from his dad and had elaborated on it. I have added my pâte brisée crust, softly roasted garlic puree, and an assortment of garden-ripe tomatoes, thinly sliced and arranged in concentric circles, with a sprinkling of grated fontina cheese. This tart is best made when the tomatoes are ripe in the garden. I serve it as a first course for dinner or a main course for lunch, straight from the oven. The tart is a very good alternative to the ubiquitous quiche and a wonderful way to add tomatoes to a menu.

SERVES 8

1. Roast the garlic: Preheat the oven to 400°F. Place the garlic on a piece of parchment-lined foil and drizzle with 2 tablespoons oil. Fold to enclose the garlic. Place on a baking sheet and roast until soft, 45 minutes to 1 hour. Remove from the oven and let cool. Raise the oven temperature to 450°F. When the garlic is cool enough to handle, using either your hands or the dull end of a large knife, squeeze the cloves out of their skins and into a small bowl; mash with a fork and set aside. Discard the papery skins.

2. On a lightly floured surface, roll out the dough to ⅛ inch thick, about 12 inches in diameter. With a dry pastry brush, brush off the excess flour. Roll the dough around the rolling pin, and lift it over a 10-inch round fluted tart pan with a removable bottom. Fit it into the tart pan. Trim the dough so that it is flush with the edges. Freeze until firm, about 15 minutes.

3. With an offset spatula, spread the roasted garlic evenly on the chilled crust. Sprinkle with half the cheese. Arrange the tomatoes on top of the cheese in an overlapping circular pattern. Season with salt and pepper. Sprinkle with the remaining cheese and the halved cherry tomatoes, if desired, and drizzle with the remaining 2 tablespoons oil.

4. Reduce the temperature to 400°F. Bake until the crust is golden and the tomatoes are soft but still retain their shape, 45 to 55 minutes. Transfer to a wire rack to cool for 20 minutes, top with thyme sprigs, and serve warm.

A LOFTY SOUFFLÉ

To demystify the lofty soufflé, we (my editors and I and the photography team Guzman) created a how-to story, utilizing all the talents and resources of a high-fashion magazine shoot. Although this photo was taken in 1993, and I was thirty-plus years younger, the makeup artist used a temporary "face-lift" method to pull back my jawline and neck so I was completely taut and lean. The designer blouse (Armani) and the wrinkled chef's apron, tied twice just like a professional chef de cuisine would do, contrast appropriately with the starched damask napkin on which the hot soufflé, right out of the oven, rests. I look like me, but different. The soufflé looks like the perfect soufflé. The step-by-step photos were exacting. And the story guaranteed a perfect result if the reader followed the well-presented recipe. I loved the fashion-shoot idea for food and recipes—a soufflé is elevated; thus, it must be treated in an elegant and beautifully lit way. My editors and I learned a lot on this photo shoot. We learned that we have to treat all food with great respect. No detail is too small. Lighting is essential and all important, and the setting has to be correct for the subject matter. I never worked with the Guzman team again like this, but their photography was formative in the look and feel of our beautiful magazine, and I treasure their photos.

Photo by Guzman, 1993

Five-Cheese Soufflé

4 tablespoons unsalted butter, cut into small cubes, plus more, softened, for the soufflé dish

1 cup plus 1 tablespoon unbleached all-purpose flour

1 tablespoon kosher salt

3⅓ cups half-and-half

6 large eggs plus 5 large egg whites, separated

5½ ounces Emmental cheese, cut into ¼-inch cubes

3½ ounces Comté cheese, cut into ¼-inch cubes

2 ounces Der scharfe Maxx cheese, cut into ¼-inch cubes

1½ ounces Appenzeller cheese, cut into ¼-inch cubes

1½ ounces Pleasant Ridge Reserve cheese, cut into ¼-inch cubes

What makes this soufflé superior are the five distinctive cheeses. These are sophisticated options that can be found at well-stocked stores like Murray's Cheese in New York City or online (I shop at the excellent Plum Plums Cheese near my home)—you'll want a good vendor who can advise on substitutions, if needed. For lunch, serve this with a fresh green salad of mâche, butter lettuce, or a mix of soft, small-leafed types. I like to pair the greens with a rich balsamic vinaigrette, and, when I have it, a thinly sliced black truffle on top. Absolute perfection.

SERVES 7

1. Preheat the oven to 400°F with a rack in the lower third (and no rack above it, to allow for rising). Butter a 7-inch round, 3¾-inch-high, 9-cup soufflé dish. Using a piece of parchment, form a collar around the soufflé dish so that it extends 3½ inches above the top of the dish; using kitchen twine, tie to secure. Place on a rimmed baking sheet and set aside.

2. In a large saucepan, whisk together the flour and salt. Gradually whisk in the half-and-half and place over medium-high heat, whisking constantly until thick and smooth.

3. Transfer to a large bowl and scatter the butter over the top. (The butter will melt and prevent a skin from forming on the surface.) Let cool until lukewarm.

4. Stir the 6 egg yolks and all the cheese into the half-and-half mixture. Set aside.

5. In the bowl of a stand mixer fitted with the whisk attachment, beat the 11 egg whites until medium to stiff peaks form. Gently fold the egg whites into the bowl with the cheese mixture. Transfer to the prepared soufflé dish.

6. Transfer to the oven and bake until the soufflé is risen and set, 40 to 45 minutes. Remove the collar and serve immediately.

Asparagus-and-Pea Risotto

6 cups Homemade Vegetable Stock (page 288) or store-bought

¼ cup extra-virgin olive oil

1 small onion, finely chopped

1 cup arborio or carnaroli rice

½ cup dry white wine

1 bunch asparagus, trimmed and cut into 2-inch pieces

1 cup fresh or frozen peas, thawed

1 ounce Parmigiano-Reggiano, finely grated on a rasp (½ cup), plus more for serving

1 teaspoon grated lemon zest plus 2 tablespoons fresh lemon juice (from 1 lemon)

Kosher salt and freshly ground pepper

Chives, snipped, for serving

Whenever I am at a loss as to what to serve, I choose one of the many risottos in my repertoire, using the very best imported arborio rice, which is from the Po Valley region of Italy. When cooked, this short-grained, high-starch-content rice remains firm, creamy, and chewy and absorbs flavors of other ingredients beautifully. In springtime, when the first of my asparagus are popping up out of the ground, I like to pick a few and make this delicious version, combining the tiny spears with the earliest garden shell peas and a generous topping of finely grated Parmigiano. A note of caution: Risotto cannot be rushed. Add the liquid as instructed, stir constantly, and don't wander out of the kitchen until the dish is done. Serve immediately for highest compliments.

SERVES 4

1. Bring the stock to a simmer in a medium saucepan.

2. Heat 2 tablespoons oil over medium in another saucepan. Cook the onion, stirring frequently, until soft, 6 to 7 minutes. Add the rice and cook, stirring, until the edges are translucent, 2 to 3 minutes. Add the wine and cook, stirring, just until evaporated.

3. Add ½ cup hot stock and cook, stirring, until almost absorbed. Continue adding ½ cup stock in this manner until the liquid is creamy and the rice is al dente, about 20 minutes total (you may not need to add all the stock). Add the asparagus with the last addition of stock, and the peas about 1 minute before the risotto is done.

4. Remove from the heat and stir in the cheese, lemon zest and juice, and remaining 2 tablespoons oil. Season with salt and pepper. Top with chives and additional cheese before serving.

MAKING PASTA

I adore this early photo of mother and daughter, me and Alexis, intently involved in the art of making pasta. We are working in our Turkey Hill kitchen, at our 1805 farmhouse in Westport, Connecticut, using the same little hand-turned Atlas pasta machine that I still use today. At the time this photo was taken, I was very involved in my catering business, yet because Alexis was so interested in cooking and the preparation of food, I hosted cooking lessons for her and several of her friends. I am doing exactly the same thing now for thirteen-year-old Jude, my granddaughter, who loves to cook as much as her mother does. Alexis was an amazingly proficient student—she is, as a result, a very fine chef, able to create pretty much anything in the kitchen. I wholeheartedly endorse teaching your children what you know and, if they wish, sending them to cooking classes.

The kitchen at Turkey Hill was a beautiful square room with a brick beehive oven, high ceilings with exposed antique ceiling joists, and all the original woodwork. To make the kitchen more utilitarian, we knocked down the back exterior wall to create a large cooking area. A wooden counter, fitted with storage drawers and cupboards, separated these two sections of the kitchen. Andy and I stripped all the paint from the beautiful pine woodwork. We built the kitchen cabinets from sycamore wood we had harvested in Massachusetts, and we laid down a beautiful dark gray slate floor. It was a true country kitchen, but totally utilitarian and large enough to cook lots of food for lots of people. A second prep kitchen was installed in the spacious old basement, where I did a lot of baking for catering, canning, and preserving. There was always a lot of activity in my kitchen—then and now.

Photo courtesy of author, late 1970s

Pasta Limone

Kosher salt

8 ounces bucatini or angel hair pasta

2 tablespoons extra-virgin olive oil

1 tablespoon unsalted butter

½ teaspoon finely grated Meyer lemon zest, plus more for serving (from 1 lemon)

3 tablespoons fresh Meyer lemon juice (from 1 lemon)

2 ounces Parmigiano-Reggiano, finely grated on a rasp (about 1 cup), plus more for serving

Caviar, for serving (optional)

With or without a generous spoonful of caviar on top, this dish has become one of my favorite pastas. We often serve it as a main course or in a much smaller portion as a first course if meat or fish is being offered. Freshly grated lemon zest (always use a very fine rasp) and just-squeezed juice from fragrant lemons—Meyer lemons are excellent—are essential, as is freshly grated Parmigiano. I prefer bucatini if this is being used as a main course and angel hair for a delicate starter.

SERVES 2

1. Bring a pot of salted water to a boil. Add the pasta and cook until slightly less than al dente, about 2 minutes less than the package instructions. Reserve 1½ cups pasta water and then drain the pasta.

2. In a large skillet, combine the oil, butter, and ½ cup pasta water. Bring the butter mixture to a simmer, swirling to melt the butter. Add the cooked pasta and toss to coat. Add the lemon zest and juice and continue stirring to create a silky sauce, adding more pasta water as needed. Add the grated cheese and toss to combine.

3. Twirl the pasta into bowls. Grate additional lemon zest and cheese over the pasta, and serve with a large dollop of caviar, if desired.

Linguine with Clams

Kosher salt and freshly
ground black pepper

12 ounces linguine

6 garlic cloves, very thinly
sliced

¼ cup extra-virgin olive
oil, plus more for
drizzling

8 ounces cherry tomatoes
(1¼ cups), halved

¼ teaspoon crushed
red-pepper flakes, plus
more for serving

1 cup dry white wine

½ cup bottled clam juice,
such as Bar Harbor

2 pounds very small
clams, such as cockles or
littlenecks

¾ cup packed coarsely
chopped fresh flat-leaf
parsley, plus more for
serving

3 tablespoons unsalted
butter, softened

1 ounce Parmigiano-
Reggiano, finely grated
on a rasp (½ cup), plus
more for serving

I love clams—on the half shell, stuffed, in chowder, and most certainly with pasta. This is a great summer luncheon dish or an easy supper to try when fresh clams are available. It will become a favorite at-home meal—not just reserved for when you visit the local Italian restaurant! I prefer to use littlenecks, and I take extra care not to overcook these small delicacies. In each of my favorite pasta recipes, I use Italian-made, high-quality dry pastas, which are available in many specialty grocers as well as online.

SERVES 4

1. Bring a large pot of salted water to a boil. Add the pasta and cook until slightly less than al dente, about 2 minutes less than the package instructions. Reserve 1 cup pasta water and then drain the pasta.

2. Meanwhile, heat the garlic with the oil in a large straight-sided skillet over medium-high until just golden brown, 2 to 3 minutes, transferring each slice to a plate when browned. Add the tomatoes and red-pepper flakes to the skillet and cook until the tomatoes soften a bit, about 3 minutes.

3. Add the wine and bring to a boil. Continue to cook until reduced by half, 1 to 2 minutes more. Add the clam juice and return to a boil. Add the clams, cover, and cook 20 seconds. Uncover and cook, using a slotted spoon to transfer the clams to a large bowl as they open, 3 to 4 minutes. (Discard any unopened clams.)

4. Add the pasta, parsley, ½ cup pasta water, and the softened butter to the skillet. Cook, stirring, until the pasta is cooked through, about 2 minutes. Remove the skillet from the heat. Add the cheese and stir, adding more pasta water as needed to create a silky sauce. Season to taste with salt and black pepper. Pour over the clams and toss to combine.

5. Divide linguine with clams among bowls and drizzle with oil. Sprinkle with garlic slices and more red-pepper flakes and parsley before serving with additional cheese on the side.

Angel Hair Pasta with Black Truffles

Kosher salt and freshly ground pepper

8 ounces angel hair pasta or thin spaghetti

4 tablespoons unsalted butter

1 black truffle (about 1 ounce), thinly sliced and then diced (a scant ½ cup)

Flaky sea salt, such as Maldon, for serving

Years ago, when Babbo was the place to eat pasta in New York, I ate a dish similar to this one and finally understood the complicated yet elusive flavor of black truffles. Very finely sliced on a truffle shaver or mandoline, then diced, the black truffles are warmed in melted unsalted butter and added to hot, just-cooked angel hair pasta. Enough butter must be used, and flaky Maldon sea salt should be sprinkled generously on top to enhance the deep flavor of the truffle. I serve this pasta with a flavorful Italian Chardonnay. Add a Bibb lettuce salad dressed with a pungent vinaigrette, and you have a delightful supper.

SERVES 2

1. Bring a pot of salted water to a boil. Add the pasta and cook until slightly less than al dente, about 2 minutes less than package instructions. Reserve 1 cup pasta water and then drain the pasta.

2. Melt the butter in a large skillet over medium heat. Add the truffle and cook until it is fragrant, about 2 minutes. Add the pasta and ¼ cup reserved pasta water. Simmer, tossing a few times, adding more pasta water as needed to create a silky sauce, until the sauce evenly coats the pasta. Season to taste with kosher salt and pepper.

3. Twirl the pasta into bowls and sprinkle with flaky sea salt before serving.

Turkey Meatballs with Spaghetti

FOR THE MEATBALLS

- 1 tablespoon extra-virgin olive oil, plus more for pan-frying
- 2 small onions, finely chopped
- 4 garlic cloves, minced
- 2 celery stalks with leaves, finely chopped

  Kosher salt and freshly ground black pepper
- ½ cup red-pepper relish (I like Fourth Creek Food Co.)
- 2 tablespoons low-sodium soy sauce
- 2 teaspoons Worcestershire sauce
- 4 large eggs
- 2 pounds ground dark meat turkey (I use Pat LaFrieda)
- 2 pounds ground light meat turkey
- ⅓ cup fresh flat-leaf parsley, finely chopped
- ½ loaf brioche, crust removed, pulsed in the food processor until fine (makes 4 cups)

I grew up next door to the Allegri family in Nutley, New Jersey. Every Saturday, the red sauce started bubbling on the stove and the meatballs were mixed and rolled—sometimes large balls, sometimes small, but always fluffy and light and very well seasoned. Lightly sautéed prior to simmering in the sauce, Mrs. Allegri's meatballs were extremely flavorful. I do not recall Mrs. Allegri ever using turkey for her meatballs, but I do think she would be proud of my recipe. One secret ingredient? The red-pepper relish.

SERVES 8 TO 10 (MAKES TEN 8-OUNCE MEATBALLS)

1. Make the meatballs: Heat the oil in a skillet over medium-high. Sauté the onions, garlic, and celery until soft, 6 to 8 minutes. Season with 1 teaspoon salt and ½ teaspoon black pepper. Add the relish and cook, stirring, until the liquid evaporates, 6 to 8 minutes. Stir in the soy sauce and Worcestershire. Transfer the relish mixture to a bowl and let cool for 5 minutes.

2. In a large bowl, whisk the eggs. Add the dark and light turkey, parsley, 1¾ cups breadcrumbs, cooled relish mixture, 1 tablespoon plus 1 teaspoon salt, and 2 teaspoons black pepper and mix until combined. Using a 1-cup scoop, form 10 meatballs (about 8 ounces each). Refrigerate for 30 minutes until chilled. Roll the meatballs in the remaining 2¼ cups breadcrumbs to coat. Cover with plastic wrap and refrigerate until chilled, at least 1 hour and up to overnight.

continued

FOR THE SAUCE

½ cup extra-virgin olive oil

6 garlic cloves, minced

6 celery stalks, finely chopped

3 medium yellow onions, finely chopped

Kosher salt and freshly ground black pepper

4 (28-ounce) cans whole peeled tomatoes, passed through the medium disc of a food mill

1 cup basil leaves

FOR SERVING

Kosher salt

2 pounds spaghetti

Freshly grated Parmigiano-Reggiano

Basil leaves

3. Meanwhile, make the sauce: In a large pot, heat the oil over medium. Add the garlic and cook until fragrant, about 1 minute. Add the celery and onions and cook, stirring occasionally, until tender, about 15 minutes. Season with 1 teaspoon salt and ½ teaspoon black pepper. Add the tomatoes and bring to a boil. Reduce to a rapid simmer and cook until slightly thickened, about 15 minutes. Season to taste with more salt and black pepper.

4. Meanwhile, pan-fry the meatballs: Heat 1 tablespoon oil in a skillet over medium. Working in batches, add the meatballs and cook until golden brown on all sides, 6 to 8 minutes. Transfer the meatballs to the tomato sauce. Add the basil leaves.

5. Bring the tomato sauce and meatballs to a rapid simmer, then reduce heat to medium-low and cook, partially covered, stirring carefully and occasionally, until the meatballs are tender and the sauce is reduced and thickened, about 1 hour 30 minutes.

6. To serve: Bring a large pot of salted water to a boil. Add the pasta and cook until slightly less than al dente, about 2 minutes less than the package instructions; drain the pasta. Twirl the spaghetti into bowls and top with meatballs and sauce. Sprinkle with cheese and basil leaves before serving.

Bucatini with Bottarga

- 2 tablespoons extra-virgin olive oil
- 1 cup coarsely ground breadcrumbs (from a baguette pulsed in a food processor)
- 4 garlic cloves, very thinly sliced
- ¼ cup drained minced capers
- 4 anchovies, finely chopped
- Grated zest and juice of 1 lemon, plus 1 lemon for serving
- 3 tablespoons coarsely chopped fresh flat-leaf parsley
- Kosher salt and freshly ground pepper
- 1 pound bucatini
- 2 tablespoons unsalted butter
- 2 tablespoons grated bottarga, plus more ungrated for serving (about 3 ounces total)

I had never had bucatini, a thick, tubular spaghetti-like pasta, prior to visiting the Italian island of Sardinia. I also had never tasted bottarga, preserved and salted mullet roe, until that very same trip. We were traveling on a motor yacht with friends, stopping here and there along the western coast of Italy. My friend Jean Pigozzi took us to visit the Parisian aristocrat Jacqueline de Ribes in Porto Ercole, and from there we sailed to Sardinia, where we were entertained by another of Jean's friends. It was that man who cooked what was the most memorable meal we had in Italy. Salty, flavorful bottarga was finely grated on a breadcrumb-and-parsley topping, infused with rich virgin olive oil, anchovies, and capers. This is my American-made version, which my family and I love.

SERVES 4 TO 6

1. Heat the oil in a skillet over medium. Add the breadcrumbs and toast, stirring frequently, until lightly browned, about 2 minutes. Push to one side and add the garlic. Cook for 30 seconds until fragrant, then stir into the breadcrumbs. Add the capers and anchovies and stir into the breadcrumbs. Remove the pan from heat and add half the lemon zest, 2 tablespoons parsley, and salt to taste.

2. Bring a pot of salted water to a boil. Add the pasta and cook until slightly less than al dente, about 2 minutes less than the package instructions. Reserve 1 cup pasta water and then drain the pasta and return to the pot.

3. Add the butter, lemon juice, remaining lemon zest, and ½ cup reserved pasta water to the pot of pasta. Cook over medium-high heat, 1 to 2 minutes, stirring frequently. Add the remaining pasta water as needed to reach the desired consistency.

4. Remove from the heat and add the grated bottarga and the remaining tablespoon parsley. Season with salt and pepper. Twirl the bucatini into bowls, sprinkle with breadcrumbs, and grate bottarga and lemon zest over top before serving.

Potato Pierogi

FOR THE DOUGH

- 1 large egg
- 2 heaping tablespoons sour cream
- 1 cup whole milk
- 4½ cups unbleached all-purpose flour, plus more for dusting

FOR THE FILLING

- 5 pounds (about 10 medium) baking potatoes, peeled and quartered
- Kosher salt and freshly ground pepper
- 8 tablespoons (1 stick) unsalted butter, melted
- 4 ounces cream cheese
- 2 ounces cheddar cheese, grated (about ½ cup), optional
- 2 tablespoons cornmeal

FOR THE SAGE BROWN BUTTER

- 12 tablespoons (1½ sticks) unsalted butter
- 30 sage leaves

Because this was my favorite thing my mother, Big Martha, made for us, I reserved an entire day years ago to spend with her so I could learn her techniques. I recorded, step-by-step, how she made her dough, created my two favorite fillings—potato and cabbage—and cooked and froze and reheated the dumplings. While we were at it, I had her re-create a sweet variation, the Italian plum pierogi. As I write this, my mouth is watering and my cravings grow. Be ready to spend a few hours on the preparation. If you can, call in a friend to help, because you'll want to make plenty—some to eat right away and the rest to freeze for later!

MAKES ABOUT 60

1. Make the dough: In a medium bowl, whisk the egg. Add the sour cream and whisk until smooth. Add the milk and 1 cup water and whisk until combined. Slowly add about 3 cups flour and stir with a wooden spoon to combine.

2. Turn the dough out onto a well-floured surface and work in about 1 cup flour as you knead. Use a bench scraper to lift the dough, as it will stick to the counter before the flour is worked in. Continue kneading for 8 to 10 minutes, working in another ½ cup flour. The dough should be elastic in texture and no longer sticky. Be careful not to add too much flour, as this will toughen the dough. Place the dough in a lightly floured bowl and cover with an inverted bowl or plastic wrap; let it rest while you prepare the filling.

3. Make the filling: Place the potatoes in a large pot and cover with cold water. Season with salt. Place over high heat and bring to a boil. Cook until fork-tender, about 30 minutes. Drain and mash with a potato masher. Add the melted butter and cheese and continue to mash until well incorporated. Season with salt and pepper to taste.

continued

4. Place a large pot of salted water over high heat and bring to a boil. Lay a clean linen towel on your counter, and evenly distribute cornmeal on it to prevent sticking.

5. On a floured surface, roll out the dough to about ⅛ inch thick. Using a glass or cookie cutter measuring 2½ inches in diameter, cut out as many circles as possible. Gather the dough scraps together, rolling them out again, and continue cutting.

6. Form the filling into 1½-inch balls and place a ball in the center of each dough circle. Holding a circle in your hand, fold the dough over the filling and pinch the edges, forming a well-sealed crescent. Transfer to the linen towel. Continue this process until all the dough circles are filled.

7. Working in batches, cook the pierogi in boiling water. They will sink to the bottom of the pot and then rise to the top. Once they rise, let them cook for about 1 minute more.

8. Meanwhile, make the sage brown butter: Heat the butter in a medium heavy-bottomed skillet over medium-high until the foam subsides and the butter begins to brown. Add the sage and cook, stirring, until the leaves are crisp and butter is golden brown.

9. Drizzle a platter with some of the brown butter. Remove the pierogi from the pot and transfer to the platter. Drizzle the pierogi with the remaining brown butter and the sage leaves, and serve.

Italian Plum Pierogi

I absolutely love this sweet pierogi! Make the pierogi dough above and then fill it with ripe Italian **plums** (you'll need 24): Cut a slit into (not through!) each plum, removing the pits. Fill the cavity of each with ¼ teaspoon **sugar**. Close the plums before wrapping them in dough. Use 1 plum for each pierogi. Cook them in boiling water, 2 to 4 minutes, depending on their ripeness. I serve them with sweetened and vanilla-flavored **sour cream**.

Mom making pierogi on our Westport kitchen set for a February 2004 MSL story entitled "Mother Knows Best."

Herb Roasted Chickens

2 (3- to 4-pound) chickens

Kosher salt and freshly ground pepper

4 (1-inch-thick) slices brioche bread, crusts removed and cubed (about 4 ounces)

14 tablespoons unsalted butter, softened

Garlic Confit (recipe follows)

2 cups fresh flat-leaf parsley, finely chopped, plus sprigs for serving

1 tablespoon fresh thyme leaves, finely chopped, plus sprigs for serving

1 teaspoon fresh rosemary needles, finely chopped, plus sprigs for serving

Garlic Confit

MAKES ½ CUP

Preheat the oven to 275°F. Using a serrated knife, remove the top third of 3 heads of **garlic**. Place cut-side down in a 6-cup loaf pan. Add 6 **thyme** sprigs and enough extra-virgin **olive oil** to cover (about 2 cups). Cover with parchment-lined foil and bake until the garlic is soft, 1 hour to 1 hour 15 minutes. Transfer to an airtight container and refrigerate up to 2 weeks.

This is one of several recipes adapted for The Bedford, my restaurant in Las Vegas, that I wanted to include in this book. My friend Pierre Schaedelin, the restaurant's consulting chef; Thomas Joseph, my culinary director; and I worked very hard to get this recipe exactly right. The stuffing that is piped under the loosened skin of young, plump, organically raised chickens is a combination of tender brioche breadcrumbs, herbs, and butter. Chilled, rubbed with softened butter, then roasted in a hot oven for about one hour, this is the chicken you will want to turn to again and again.

SERVES 8 TO 12

1. Place the chickens on a baking sheet, loosen the skin, season with salt, and refrigerate, uncovered, overnight to dry out the skin.

2. Place the brioche cubes in a food processor and pulse into fine crumbs; set aside. (You should have about 3 cups.) In a medium bowl, mix 12 tablespoons of the butter, the garlic confit, parsley, thyme, rosemary, ½ teaspoon salt, and ¼ teaspoon pepper until well combined. Add the breadcrumbs to the herbed butter and mix to combine. Transfer to a piping bag. (This can be made up to 1 day in advance and stored in the refrigerator. Bring to room temperature before piping.)

3. Carefully stretch out the chicken skin and pipe the butter-breadcrumb mixture under the skin, cutting back side skin as needed. Massage into an even layer over the breast.

Season the inside of the chickens with a little salt and pepper. Truss the chicken legs using butcher's twine. Tie the twine in a bow (it will be easier to untie later) and chill the chickens, uncovered, in the refrigerator at least 1 hour before roasting.

4. Preheat the oven to 400°F. Place a wire rack over a parchment-lined baking sheet. Rub the chickens with the remaining 2 tablespoons butter and place on the rack. Roast for 1 hour or until the internal temperature reaches 165°F in the thickest part of the legs. Tent with foil as needed if getting too brown. Remove from the oven and serve on a platter garnished with fresh herbs.

Mahogany Fried Chicken

10 cups ice water, for soaking

Kosher salt and freshly ground black pepper

2 (2½- to 3-pound) fryer chickens, each cut into 8 pieces

1 quart buttermilk

2 teaspoons cayenne pepper

2 cups unbleached all-purpose flour

Safflower oil, rice bran oil, or Crisco shortening, for frying

Dill sprigs, for serving

Simmered Asparagus (page 205), for serving

So much time has passed since I visited a family of beef-cattle ranchers in San Antonio, Texas, and learned how to make the most juicy, succulent, and crispy fried chicken. The family's housekeepers enjoyed getting together on their days off and making huge batches of chicken and all the fixings, and I was invited to watch, learn—and eat the best fried chicken I had ever had. The following is their recipe, and every time I make it my friends swoon and ask for more! Please do not eliminate the step of soaking the chicken pieces overnight in salt water, and the second overnight soaking in cayenne-flavored buttermilk. These clarify the chicken meat and ensure a delicious juiciness. You will be very happy with the results.

MAKES 16 PIECES

1. In a large bowl, stir together the ice water and 2 tablespoons salt. Add the chicken, submerging all the pieces. Cover and let soak overnight in the refrigerator.

2. The next day, in another large bowl, stir together the buttermilk, 1 tablespoon salt, and 1 teaspoon cayenne; add the chicken, turning to coat. Cover with plastic wrap and refrigerate for at least 6 hours and up to overnight.

3. In a large brown paper bag, combine the flour with the remaining 1 teaspoon cayenne, plus 1 teaspoon salt and 1 tablespoon black pepper; shake to combine. Working one at a time, place the chicken pieces in the bag and shake to coat. Place the coated pieces on a clean tray.

4. Fill a large, deep, straight-sided skillet, such as a cast-iron, slightly less than halfway with oil, and heat the oil to 350°F. Using tongs, add the chicken one piece at a time, being careful not to overcrowd pan. Fry, turning every 3 to 4 minutes, until deep mahogany in color, about 18 minutes. Remove the chicken from the skillet and drain on a brown paper bag. Transfer to a platter, top with dill, and serve hot, warm, or cold with a side of asparagus.

Sugar-and-Tea-Smoked Chicken

1 (3½- to 4-pound) roasting chicken or 3 Cornish hens

3 to 4 pounds kosher salt

1 cup sugar

1 to 2 tablespoons smoky tea (Lapsang Souchong or Hu-Kwa)

5 star anise pods

1 to 2 tablespoons fresh herbs (optional)

Lettuce leaves, for serving

Horseradish Sauce (recipe follows), for serving

I first introduced this delectable smoked chicken recipe in 1984, in *Martha Stewart's Hors d'Oeuvres*. I had learned the recipe from food journalist and author Brooke Dojny, who had learned it from a friend. The process is a bit involved, but the result is amazingly delicious and unusual. It begins with a plump 3½-pound hen, preferably organically grown, and a dry-brine of kosher salt for three days. The chicken is then rinsed, trussed tightly, poached for about ten minutes, and smoked over a mixture of sugar and smoky Chinese tea—Lapsang Souchong is perfect—in a specially prepared pan on a rack. My pan fits two chickens nicely, so I often cook two at once. The result is surprisingly beautiful, mahogany skin, white tender meat, and a delicate, unusually good smoky flavor.

SERVES 12 TO 15

1. Wash the chicken. Fill the cavity with salt. Add some salt to a stainless-steel or glass bowl that is just large enough to hold the chicken. Place the chicken on top of the salt, and then pour on additional salt almost to cover. Cover the bowl with plastic wrap and refrigerate for 3 days. If you are doing more than one chicken, put them in the same bowl and cover with salt.

2. After 3 days, rinse the chicken under cold running water, making sure to rinse out all the salt in the cavity. Truss the chicken tightly with cotton twine or butcher string, folding the wing tips under the breasts.

3. Bring a large Dutch oven of water to a boil, immerse the chicken, and simmer over medium-low heat for 20 minutes. (Simmer hens for 10 to 12 minutes.) Drain well on a rack.

continued

Choose an old, heavy steel or cast-iron roasting pan for smoking. Mine is big enough to hold two chickens, so I often just double this recipe and smoke two. Once used, the pan is best reserved just for smoking. To wash it, soak the pan in very hot water. Use just steel wool, no soap.

4. Line a very heavy roasting pan, with a tight-fitting cover, with aluminum foil. Sprinkle the foil with the sugar, tea, star anise, and herbs, if desired. Set a rack inside the roasting pan and put the chicken on the rack. (If smoking more than one chicken or hen, do not crowd them in the pan.) Cover the pan tightly and set it on the stove over the highest heat. Turn on the kitchen exhaust fan. Leave the pan over the heat for 30 minutes. Do not open the pan before the time is up. Turn off the heat and let the pot cool for 20 minutes.

5. Use tongs or a long fork to remove the chicken from the pan. Be very careful not to break the skin. Drain the cavity over the sink and let the chicken cool on a rack. The skin will be a dark mahogany color.

6. To slice the chicken, carefully disjoint the wings and whole legs, and slice the breast meat, always keeping a bit of skin on each slice. Slice the meat from legs. Leave the wings whole. The chicken is best sliced 2 to 3 days after smoking and will keep well wrapped in the refrigerator up to a week. Serve sliced on a platter with lettuce leaves and horseradish sauce.

Horseradish Sauce
MAKES ABOUT 1 CUP

Whisk 1 cup **heavy cream**, 1 tablespoon **sugar**, 2 teaspoons fresh **lemon juice**, and 1 tablespoon grated fresh or prepared **horseradish** to stiff peaks.

TURKEYS THROUGH THE YEARS

Our quest for the very best turkey roasting method began early in the evolution of *Martha Stewart Living,* my beautiful magazine, first published in 1990. Every November issue was devoted, of course, to the celebration of one of our nation's most important holidays, Thanksgiving. We took the celebration of every holiday seriously, and throughout the year we created original recipes, table settings, decorations for inside and outside the home, as well as articles on the history of the holidays in the appropriate issues. We never tired of coming up with new ideas, we never feared that we would run out of original creative concepts and content. That is why every holiday issue was a bestseller, why covers with a beautifully roasted turkey, or a giant chocolate turkey made in an antique mold, sold out every November. One spring, five months before we were to publish our November 2006 issue, we decided to celebrate Thanksgiving in the gorgeous stone stable on my farm, with my Friesian horses in residence in their stalls. It was a beautiful shoot and a memorable meal, with close friends who loved being included. They had an opportunity to experience a fine meal replete with new and delicious recipes despite the out-of-season actuality of the event. For me and my editors, the creative process never became old or trite or difficult—we found the challenges exciting, and the process enlightening and creative beyond measure. And that is something I will always be thankful for.

Photo by Earl Carter, 2006

Roasted Turkey in Parchment with Brioche Stuffing

1 (14-pound) turkey, neck and heart reserved for Homemade Turkey Stock (page 287)

Kosher salt and freshly ground pepper

10 cups Brioche Stuffing (recipe follows)

1 slice white bread, crusts removed

6 tablespoons unsalted butter, softened

Simple Turkey Gravy (recipe follows), for serving

MARTHA'S NOTE

If your turkey is larger than the 14-pounder called for in the recipe:

1. Increase length of parchment sheets so you have enough to come up and over the turkey and to crimp and staple.

2. Increase cooking time to 10 minutes more per pound before removing the parchment. Begin checking the breast temperature 30 minutes after removing parchment.

This year, we wrapped a butter-slathered, stuffed turkey in an envelope of parchment. Unwrapped after a relatively short roast, the succulent bird browns gloriously and results in perhaps the best turkey we have tasted. Most of us have tried cooking fish and even chicken "en papillote"; usually with delicious results. Well, rest-assured, sealing a large turkey in parchment with staples (or needle and thread, if necessary) is just as delicious and well worth the effort.

SERVES 8 TO 10

1. Let the turkey stand at room temperature for 1 hour. Preheat the oven to 325°F with a rack in the lower third. Pat the turkey dry with paper towels. Season the body cavity with salt and pepper and fill with about 8 cups stuffing. Fill the neck cavity with about 2 cups stuffing (amount will depend on its capacity). Slide the bread under the skin but over the stuffing, in the neck cavity. Secure the skin flaps with toothpicks or skewers. Spread 6 tablespoons butter all over the turkey, then season with salt and pepper. Tie the drumsticks together with kitchen twine. Tuck the wings under the turkey.

2. Place a 40-inch sheet of parchment on a work surface. Place the turkey on top, with a short side of the bird facing you. Gather the ends and wrap the turkey. Fold the overlapping ends of the parchment over the turkey and secure with staples. Place a 48-inch sheet of parchment on a work surface, place the turkey on top, and rotate 90 degrees. Fold the short parchment sides over the turkey and secure with staples. Rotate the bird another 90 degrees and repeat the process with another 40-inch sheet of parchment. Secure all paper flaps with staples.

3. Place the wrapped turkey on a (not a V-shaped) rack set inside a roasting pan. Roast for 2 hours and 45 minutes. Remove from the oven and cut open the parchment with scissors. Increase the oven to 425°F. While holding drumsticks, slide the parchment out and discard. Return the turkey to the oven. Continue to roast until golden brown and a thermometer inserted into the breast reads 165°F, about 45 minutes more. Transfer to a carving board and let rest at least 45 minutes and up to 1 hour before carving. Reserve the drippings in the pan for the turkey gravy.

continued

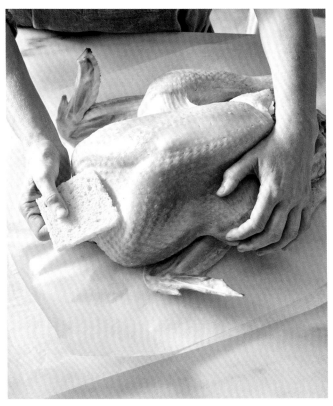

1½ pounds brioche, cut into 1-inch cubes (about 14 cups)

12 tablespoons unsalted butter

2 large onions, chopped (about 4½ cups)

2 medium leeks, white and light green parts, thinly sliced into half-moons, and washed well (about 4½ cups)

4 to 5 celery stalks, chopped (2¼ cups)

1 pound apples (about 2), peeled and cut into ½-inch cubes (3 cups)

1 pound pears (2 to 3), peeled and cut into ½-inch cubes (3 cups)

Kosher salt and freshly ground pepper

3 to 4 tablespoons chopped fresh sage

1¼ to 2 cups Homemade Vegetable Stock (page 288) or store-bought

2 large eggs

½ cup chopped fresh flat-leaf parsley

2 teaspoons Bell's All-Natural Seasoning

MARTHA'S NOTE

If you don't have time to dry the bread overnight, bake it in a preheated 350°F oven until crisp but not golden, about 10 minutes.

Brioche Stuffing

This recipe for brioche bread stuffing is very tasty and definitely a must for the Thanksgiving table. If you prefer cooking the stuffing separately, try roasting it in a shallow pumpkin for an attractive seasonal presentation. Baste it often with broth to help cook the pumpkin and stuffing evenly.

MAKES ABOUT 16 CUPS

1. Spread the bread onto 2 rimmed baking sheets and let dry overnight.

2. In a 14-inch straight-sided skillet (or 2 large skillets), melt the butter over medium-high heat. Add the onions, leeks, celery, apples, and pears. Season with salt and pepper. Cook, stirring occasionally, until the vegetables and fruit are softened and start to turn golden, about 15 minutes. Stir in the sage and cook 1 minute more.

3. Place the bread cubes in a large bowl. Add the vegetable mixture and toss well. Drizzle about 1¼ cups stock over the mixture, add the eggs, parsley, and Bell's All-Natural Seasoning, and toss to combine. If the mixture seems dry, add more stock, ¼ cup at a time. Season with 2 teaspoons salt and ½ teaspoon pepper. Use 10 cups stuffing to fill the turkey; place the remainder in a buttered 8-inch-square baking dish. After the turkey is out of the oven, lower the oven temperature to 350°F. Bake the stuffing until heated through and top is browned, 40 to 45 minutes.

Simple Turkey Gravy
MAKES ABOUT 2½ CUPS

Pour the **drippings** from the roasting pan into a fat separator and set aside. Place the pan on two burners over medium-high heat. When the pan is hot, pour in ½ cup dry **white wine**, scraping up any brown bits with a wooden spoon. Pour in the defatted drippings and 2 cups **Homemade Turkey Stock** (page 287); bring to a boil. Combine another ½ cup stock and 2 tablespoons **Wondra flour** in a small jar, seal it, and shake to combine. Pour the flour mixture into the boiling mixture in the pan and boil until thickened, 2 to 3 minutes. Pour through a fine-mesh sieve into a bowl. Reheat when ready to serve. Before serving, season with **salt** and freshly ground **pepper**.

Duck Breast with Sour Cherry Sauce

4 (11-ounce) duck breasts

Kosher salt and freshly ground pepper

Sour Cherry Sauce (recipe follows), for serving

Persian Rice (*Tahdig*, page 218), for serving

I fondly recall the superb roast whole duck carved and served tableside in the Philip Johnson–designed dining room of the original Four Seasons restaurant, in New York City's iconic Seagram Building. I must have ordered that dish at least four or six times a year, reveling in the rich sour cherry sauce and the tender Muscovy duck with its crispy skin. That, a Bibb lettuce salad, and a Grand Marnier soufflé was one of my favorite meals. When I planted my first fruit orchard at Turkey Hill, I included six Montmorency cherry trees, sourcing them from the wonderful Henry Leuthardt Nurseries on eastern Long Island. The trees provided me with many quarts of the proper cherries for this sauce and for sour cherry pies. I now have even more sour cherry trees on my farm in Bedford and pick, pit, and freeze as many quarts as I can to always have such cherries on hand. Frozen sour cherries are also available in specialty-food stores. It is important to score the skin of the duck breasts the night before and salt and pepper them. Refrigerate, uncovered, before cooking them as directed.

SERVES 4

1. Score the skin of each duck breast in a diamond pattern. (This will help the fat render faster.) Season with salt and pepper, and arrange in a single layer on a baking sheet. Refrigerate, uncovered, overnight. Let come to room temperature for 1 hour before cooking.

2. Preheat the oven to 250°F. Arrange the seasoned breasts, fat-side down, in a cold heavy-bottomed, oven-safe skillet. Place over medium-low heat and cook, undisturbed, until the fat is evenly rendered and golden brown, about 15 to 20 minutes. Pour off the rendered fat, as needed.

3. Transfer the skillet to the oven and cook for 10 minutes for medium-rare (135°F), or until the desired temperature. Remove from the oven and place the duck breasts fat-side up on a cutting board. Let them rest at least 10 minutes before slicing. Slice and season with salt. Serve with the sour cherry sauce and Persian rice on the side.

Sour Cherry Sauce

SERVES 4

In a saucepan, combine 1 quart **Homemade Chicken Stock** (page 287) or store-bought, 6 **thyme** sprigs, 1 teaspoon **black peppercorns**, 1 peeled and quartered **shallot**, ⅓ cup freshly squeezed **orange juice**, and 2 tablespoons **red wine vinegar**. Bring to a boil over medium-high heat. Reduce the heat to a simmer and continue to cook until the liquid has reduced to ¾ cup, 18 to 20 minutes. Strain, discard the solids, and return the liquid to the pan. Stir in 1 cup frozen pitted **sour cherries** and 1 tablespoon cold **unsalted butter,** cut into small pieces, swirling the pan over low heat until combined. Remove from the heat and season with **salt**. (Store in an airtight container up to 1 week.)

Paella

12 bone-in, skin-on
    chicken thighs (about
    5 pounds)

3   tablespoons olive oil

2   teaspoons sweet paprika

4   large tomatoes

1   large red bell pepper,
    seeded, deveined, and
    cut into quarters

1   large green bell pepper,
    seeded, deveined, and
    cut into quarters

2   teaspoons saffron

    Kosher salt and freshly
    ground pepper

4   cups Homemade Chicken
    Stock (page 287) or
    store-bought, warmed

⅓   cup cognac

continued

My first visit to northern Spain was when I was seventeen. My mother was accompanying my middle sister, Kathy, to Santander for an intense Spanish language class, and I joined them by train from Paris for the journey. We ate and laughed our way to Spain, where I experienced my first paella, cooked al fresco in a magnificent steel pan, forty inches or so in diameter, over a wood fire. I actually wrote the steps down, timing the cooking and stirring of each ingredient as the paella was assembled. It was utterly awe-inspiring. Years later, I was treated to another paella at the home of a friend who had studied in Spain and had learned how to cook a version on her stovetop, in a large two-handled steel paella pan about twenty-four inches in diameter. She often made it for guests, and we oohed and aahed over the taste, the texture of the rice, and the deliciousness of the dish. When I make this paella for my friends, it receives accolades. We published it in the magazine, we created a version of it outdoors for our television show, and it became the staple of my Maine outdoor entertaining, where it is often served for my birthday celebration in August.

SERVES 12

1. Place the chicken in a large bowl and add 2 tablespoons oil. Sprinkle with the paprika; turn the chicken to coat. Cover and let marinate, refrigerated, for at least 4 hours and up to overnight.

2. Bring a large pot of water to a boil; meanwhile, prepare an ice bath. With a paring knife, core the tomatoes and score an X on the bottoms. Working in batches, carefully lower them into the boiling water; when the skins begin to split, after 30 to 60 seconds, use a slotted spoon to transfer the tomatoes to the ice bath.

3. When the tomatoes are cool, remove the skins (using a paring knife, if necessary) and discard. Halve the tomatoes. Remove the seeds with a spoon and discard. Finely chop the tomatoes; set aside. Cut the peppers crosswise and into ¼-inch strips; set aside.

4. Using a mortar and pestle, grind together the saffron and 1 teaspoon salt. Transfer the saffron mixture to a medium bowl. Add 1 cup chicken stock and the cognac and whisk until well combined; set aside.

continued

MARTHA'S NOTE

The secrets for successful paella are as follows: A large grill that will accommodate a hot, hardwood fire. A large pan slightly smaller in diameter than the diameter of the fire—so that the flames can reach up the outside edges of the pan, cooking the contents well and quickly, and ensuring the rice is done on time. Ingredients that are complementary and prepared in place—mise en place, as the French say. And a flaming of good cognac or Armagnac at the very end of cooking!

Paella

1   **pound pork tenderloin, trimmed and cut into 1-inch cubes**

1   **large white onion, chopped**

2   **tablespoons minced garlic**

2   **links Spanish chorizo (fresh, not dried), sliced ½ inch thick on a bias**

1¼   **pounds calamari, cleaned and cut crosswise into ½-inch rings**

12   **jumbo shrimp, peeled and deveined, with tails intact**

1¼   **pounds short-grain white rice, such as bomba**

16   **littleneck clams, scrubbed**

18   **mussels, scrubbed and debearded**

2   **cups fresh or frozen peas**

½   **cup fresh flat-leaf parsley, chopped, for serving**

    Lemon wedges, for serving

5. If using a charcoal grill, make a fire in the grill. When charcoals are completely covered in gray ash, hold your hand about 5 inches above grill grid; count how many seconds you can comfortably leave it there. When you can hold it there for only 1 to 2 seconds, you have high heat and are ready to cook. Alternatively, you can cook paella on a stove over high heat.

6. Heat an 18- to 22-inch paella pan with at least 2-inch sides over the hot grill. Coat the bottom of the pan with the remaining tablespoon of oil. Season the chicken thighs with salt and pepper and add to the pan. Cook, turning, until golden brown on all sides, about 8 minutes. Season the pork and add to the pan. Cook, turning, until browned, about 6 minutes more. Add reserved tomatoes and peppers, the onion, garlic, and chorizo. Cook, stirring, about 8 minutes. Add the calamari and shrimp, and cook, stirring, about 2 minutes more.

7. Add the rice to the pan and stir to coat. Add the reserved saffron mixture and let cook about 1 minute. Add 1½ cups more stock and bring to a boil. Cook, rotating the pan and stirring occasionally, about 15 minutes. If the rice appears dry around the edges, add more stock as necessary. Nestle the clams, mussels, and peas into the rice and add 1 cup stock. Cook, stirring occasionally, adding more stock as necessary (you may not need to use all the stock), until the rice is tender, the shellfish have opened, and nearly all the liquid has evaporated from the pan, about 20 minutes. (Discard any shellfish that have not opened.)

8. Continue to cook, without stirring, until the remaining liquid has evaporated, about 5 minutes. Season with salt. Garnish with the parsley, squeeze some lemon on top, and serve immediately with additional lemon wedges.

Black-Pepper Mussels

1½ **pounds mussels,**
scrubbed and debearded

2 **teaspoons freshly**
ground pepper

Extra-virgin olive oil, for
drizzling

Finely chopped parsley,
for serving

Lemon wedges, for
serving

When I lived at Turkey Hill, one of my favorite neighborhood restaurants and fresh pasta shops was Pasta Nostra, located in nearby South Norwalk, Connecticut. The owner-chef, Joe Bruno, was a real talent and an entrepreneur. I loved his grandmother's eggplant dish and his wonderfully made organic pastas, his lasagna, and his salads. But what really appealed to me was the extremely simple and effective way he and his colleague, Liana DiMeglio, who brought the recipe over from Naples, Italy, cooked mussels. The recipe called for just three main ingredients: pristine mussels, freshly ground black pepper, and water. Eaten hot right out of the pan—sprinkled with chopped parsley and lemon, and accompanied with buttered, toasted Italian bread—these mussels rival those of the best bistros in Paris and New York.

SERVES 2

1. Place the mussels and ¼ cup water in a large skillet. Season with 1 teaspoon pepper. Cover and cook over high heat, stirring once, until the mussels open, 2 to 3 minutes. (Discard any unopened mussels.)

2. Transfer the mussels to a serving bowl. Season with the remaining teaspoon of pepper and drizzle with oil. Garnish with parsley and serve immediately with lemon wedges.

Soft-Shell Crabs Tempura-Style

FOR THE SOFT-SHELL CRABS

1½ cups cake flour, sifted

1 tablespoon kosher salt

½ teaspoon freshly ground pepper

6 soft-shell crabs, cleaned

1½ cups rice bran oil or safflower oil

3 lemons, halved

FOR THE PONZU DIPPING SAUCE

3 tablespoons freshly grated ginger

3 tablespoons freshly grated daikon

Very thinly sliced scallions

⅔ cup dashi

Onion Rings (page 214; optional), for serving

Each spring, my colleague and best friend, Kevin Sharkey, and I eagerly await the appearance of soft-shell crabs at our favorite sushi restaurant, Sushi Yasuda. They are carefully prepared tempura-style, served cut into quarters with a small amount of dashi, grated radish, minced scallion greens, and a mound of sea salt. In this recipe, I have attempted to reproduce the crispness and tenderness of that crab. For a casual dinner, serve these soft-shell crabs with the best onion rings, homemade ponzu dipping sauce, and ice-cold beer. As the wonders of Japanese home cooking are discovered by more, it is delightful and exciting to practice one's favorite dishes, like tempura, as well as sushi and miso cod and eggplant. "Playing" Nobu or Masa (two of the most acclaimed great Japanese chefs) is not simple, but it's a very good thing!

MAKES 6 CRABS

1. Make the soft-shell crabs: In a shallow dish, season the flour with the salt and pepper. Dredge the crabs in the seasoned flour mixture, covering thoroughly; shake off any excess.

2. Heat the oil in a 3-inch-deep pan to 355°F. Fry the crabs, two at a time, until golden and crisp, 2 to 3 minutes per side. Remove to a rack to drain before serving.

3. Make the ponzu dipping sauce: In a small bowl, combine the ginger, daikon, and scallions. Add the dashi and mix until combined.

4. Serve the soft-shell crabs with ponzu dipping sauce and onion rings, if desired.

Honey-Mustard Salmon

FOR THE SHALLOT CONFIT

20 shallots

Safflower oil

FOR THE SALMON

½ cup honey

½ cup Dijon mustard

8 (7-ounce) pieces salmon fillet

Kosher salt and freshly ground pepper

Flat-leaf parsley sprigs, for serving

Wilted Spinach (page 204), for serving

This is one of the simplest and most appealing recipes you will ever make. The secrets: the freshest, best line-caught salmon; imported Dijon mustard; and fragrant wild honey. Brush a generous amount of the honey mustard on each piece of lightly salted and peppered fish. I use a salamander (an open broiler) for best results, but any broiler will do—just leave the door ajar for air circulation. Use medium-high heat and lightly brown the fillets, being careful not to burn them. Depending on the size of the fillets, seven to nine minutes is enough for medium-rare, perfectly cooked fish. The confit of shallots is an excellent side dish, as is lightly steamed fresh spinach leaves. Your family will gobble this up, so make plenty.

SERVES 8

1. Make the shallot confit: Peel the shallots and place in a small saucepan. Cover with oil and cook over low heat until the shallots become very soft and translucent, about 1 hour. (The shallot confit can be refrigerated in an airtight container up to 2 weeks.)

2. Make the salmon: Preheat the broiler to medium-high. In a small bowl or cup, mix together the honey and mustard. Season the salmon with salt and pepper. Brush each piece with 1 tablespoon honey-mustard glaze. Place the salmon on a foil-lined baking sheet. Place in the broiler and cook, brushing with more glaze halfway through, until just a bit translucent in center, 7 to 9 minutes.

3. Place the salmon and shallot confit on a platter and garnish with parsley sprigs. Serve with spinach on the side.

Hake Burgers

2½ pounds skinless hake or cod

2 large eggs

⅓ cup plus ½ cup mayonnaise

1½ cups fresh breadcrumbs (from 3 slices of crustless white bread)

¼ cup drained capers, coarsely chopped

¼ cup snipped chives

Kosher salt

Pinch of cayenne pepper

2 tablespoons Dijon mustard

2 tablespoons extra-virgin olive oil, plus more for brushing

8 brioche buns, split

Quick-Pickled Red Onions (recipe follows)

Watercress leaves, for serving

I rarely eat burgers, but this recipe has changed my idea about them. A sustainable, deep-water, non-oily fish, hake is tasty, rich in essential fatty acids, and perfect for the burger format. I cook these burgers in a hot skillet and serve them on soft brioche buns with pickled red onions, watercress, and a simple mayonnaise-mustard sauce. Hake burgers will quickly become a staple on your menu!

SERVES 8

1. Cut the fish into ¼-inch cubes. In a medium bowl, lightly beat the eggs. Add the fish, ⅓ cup mayonnaise, the breadcrumbs, capers, chives, 1 teaspoon salt, and the cayenne, and gently mix until combined. Form into 8 burger patties, each about 3½ inches in diameter. Refrigerate, covered, for at least 1 hour and up to 8 hours.

2. Combine the remaining ½ cup mayonnaise and the mustard in a small bowl. Set aside.

3. Heat 1 tablespoon oil in a large, heavy skillet over medium-high. Cook 4 burgers, flipping once, until golden brown and cooked through, about 10 minutes. Repeat with the remaining oil and burgers. Wipe the skillet clean, reduce the heat to medium, and return the skillet to the stove.

4. Brush the split sides of the buns with oil and lightly toast them in the skillet. Sandwich the burgers in the toasted buns and serve with the mayonnaise mixture, pickled red onions, and watercress.

Quick-Pickled Red Onions

MAKES 2 CUPS

Place 2 small thinly sliced **red onions** in a medium heatproof bowl. Bring 1 cup unseasoned **rice vinegar**, 2 tablespoons **sugar**, and 1 tablespoon kosher **salt** to a boil in a saucepan; pour the pickling liquid over the onions. Let cool completely. Refrigerate, covered, for at least 2 hours and up to 1 month.

Seared Lamb Chops

12 small lamb rib chops, frenched

Kosher salt and freshly ground pepper

Olive oil

1 mint sprig, plus more for serving

2 thyme sprigs

2 rosemary sprigs

5 garlic cloves

1 bunch scallions, trimmed, for serving

Mint jelly, for serving

Four-Root Puree (page 198), for serving

Pierre Schaedelin—a world-class chef, trained by Alain Ducasse, and a former chef at Le Cirque—came to work for me around 2005. I was so lucky to meet such an accomplished chef, and over the past nineteen years, we have collaborated hundreds of times: He made multiple appearances on *The Martha Stewart Show*, he helped develop recipes for my restaurant, and we've entertained countless friends and business colleagues, serving my guests extraordinary food while introducing them to my homegrown vegetables and beautifully sourced meats and condiments. Both Pierre and I search out the finest ingredients, oftentimes changing a menu if, for example, the celeriac is not good or the correct chickens are not available. Once the best ingredients are sourced, the best techniques are employed to ensure excellent results. These lamb chops perfectly illustrate how a simple yet superior cooking method yields the tastiest results. Follow the cooking instructions and you will be thrilled. I can easily devour three or four of these baby chops—you will, too!

SERVES 6

Pierre Schaedelin and me in 2011, at my peony garden party.

1. Preheat the oven to 450°F. Season the lamb generously with salt and pepper. Heat a layer of oil in a large, heavy skillet over medium-high until shimmering. Add the lamb chops and cook until golden brown, 1 to 2 minutes per side. Transfer the chops to a rimmed baking sheet.

2. To the skillet with oil, add the mint, thyme, rosemary, and garlic and cook until fragrant, about 30 seconds. Add to the baking sheet with the chops. Transfer to the oven and cook until medium-rare (130°F to 135°F on an instant-read thermometer), 4 to 8 minutes.

3. Heat the same skillet over medium-high. Add 1 tablespoon oil. Add the scallions and season with salt. Sauté until lightly browned, about 5 minutes. Place the lamb chops on a platter with the scallions and garlic. Garnish with mint and serve with jelly and Four-Root Puree.

Broiled Strip Steak with Bordelaise Sauce

6 boneless strip steaks, each 8 to 10 ounces and 1½ inches thick

Kosher salt and freshly ground pepper

Extra-virgin olive oil, for drizzling

Bordelaise Sauce (recipe follows), for serving

Prepared Horseradish (recipe follows), for serving

Blanched Green Beans (page 204), for serving

MARTHA'S NOTE

I prefer a nicely marbled New York strip for this dish, but you can use a filet mignon, or feed the crowd with a large boneless rib eye—just make sure the meat is about 1½ inches thick.

Every cook should be able to serve a perfect steak. An excellent piece of meat, a few simple steps, a broiler, and voilà, a steak to write home about. It starts with the meat: I prefer a smallish steak, and I find that a well-trimmed boneless prime strip is a good one-person serving. I often get my steaks from Hemlock Hill Farm in New York, where the cattle are locally raised, slaughtered on the premises, and sold directly on the farm. The strip steaks are tender, cook quickly, and have excellent flavor. Another source is Pat LaFrieda, a well-known meat purveyor in the New York area. His steaks are memorable, expensive, and worth every penny if you want the very best meat you have ever tasted. I season the meat with salt and freshly ground pepper and a rubbing of olive oil. I like to slip my steaks into my open-air broiler (a closed in-stove broiler can be used with the door ajar) until cooked to the appropriate doneness, which comes with practice and careful timing. Let the meat rest for a few minutes before slicing against the grain. I sometimes melt a small pat of butter on the steak before serving it with a lovely Bordelaise sauce.

SERVES 6 TO 12

1. Bring the steaks to room temperature, about 1 hour. Preheat the broiler on high for 5 minutes, with an oven rack in the second position from top. Line a baking sheet with aluminum foil and top with a rack.

2. Pat the steaks dry with paper towels. Using a sharp knife, score the steaks on the diagonal about ½ inch apart. Season on both sides with salt and pepper and drizzle with oil. Broil the steaks, with the oven door cracked open, 5 to 7 minutes for medium-rare (a thermometer inserted horizontally into center of the meat should register 125°F), rotating the pan and flipping the steaks halfway through. Transfer the steaks to a warm plate to rest, about 5 minutes. Serve with the Bordelaise sauce, prepared horseradish, and green beans on the side.

continued

2 tablespoons extra-virgin olive oil, plus more if needed

2 pounds stew beef, cut into 1- to 2-inch pieces

Kosher salt and freshly ground pepper

2 yellow onions, chopped

2 cups dry red wine, such as Bordeaux

6 cups Homemade Vegetable Stock (page 288) or store-bought

1 tablespoon unsalted butter

2 small shallots, minced

1 tablespoon cornstarch

Bordelaise Sauce

This classic, rich French sauce is traditionally made with a full-bodied wine from the region of Bordeaux, but you can substitute any good-quality dry red wine.

MAKES 2 CUPS

1. In a large stockpot, heat the oil over medium-high. Season the stew beef with salt and pepper. Add the stew beef to the pot and cook, stirring occasionally, until browned on all sides, about 20 minutes. (If the stew beef is not fatty, add additional oil to sear it properly.) Add the onions and cook until caramelized, about 5 minutes. Add 1 cup red wine and bring to a boil for 1 minute. Add the vegetable stock and bring to a boil. Reduce heat, cover, and simmer on low until the meat is tender and starts to fall apart, 1 to 2 hours.

2. Remove the pot from the heat and allow it to cool slightly. Using a fine-mesh strainer set over a liquid measuring cup, strain the liquid and discard the beef. Set aside the beef stock.

3. Heat the butter in a small pot over medium. Sauté the shallots until softened, 3 to 4 minutes. Season with salt and pepper. Add the remaining cup of red wine and reduce completely, 6 to 7 minutes. Pour 2 cups reserved beef stock over the shallots and reduce until almost coating the back of a wooden spoon, about 10 minutes.

4. In a small bowl, mix together the cornstarch and 2 tablespoons water to create a slurry. Add the mixture to the sauce to thicken it to the desired consistency. Season with salt.

Prepared Horseradish

MAKES 1½ CUPS

Chop 12 ounces peeled **horseradish root** into ½-inch pieces. Place in the bowl of a food processor with 2 tablespoons **sugar**, 1 tablespoon plus 1½ teaspoons unseasoned **rice vinegar**, and 1 tablespoon kosher **salt**. Puree until finely minced and well combined, about 1 minute. (Store prepared horseradish in the refrigerator, in an airtight container, for up to 2 weeks.)

JULIA & JACQUES

ONE OF THE BEST THINGS about having done so many television shows are the guests whom I have worked with, interviewed, and learned from. I adore this photo of two of my heroes in the kitchen, the inimitable Julia Child and her colleague and friend Jacques Pépin. In 1999, they came on my show to discuss their book, *Julia and Jacques Cooking at Home*, and to cook Chateaubriand with béarnaise sauce. I learned a lot that day—it was inevitable—and we had so much fun! Both Julia and Jacques were instrumental in teaching the art of French cookery to the American public. Both were prolific writers and television personalities. Julia, of course, made French cuisine understandable and important, and extremely desirable for all of us in the United States who wanted to elevate our skills and taste buds. Jacques was trained in France, had been the personal chef to Charles de Gaulle, and moved to the US in 1959, working first at New York's historic Le Pavillon restaurant. They provided all of us with workable recipes and clear directions. No longer did we think that boeuf bourguignon was only to be eaten in French restaurants, and no longer was the French baguette to be made only in a French bakery. Julia and Jacques both visited me in Westport, at Turkey Hill, and Jacques recently appeared on my Roku show, demonstrating his foolproof method for perfectly roasted chicken, something we all want and need!

Photo courtesy of author, 1999

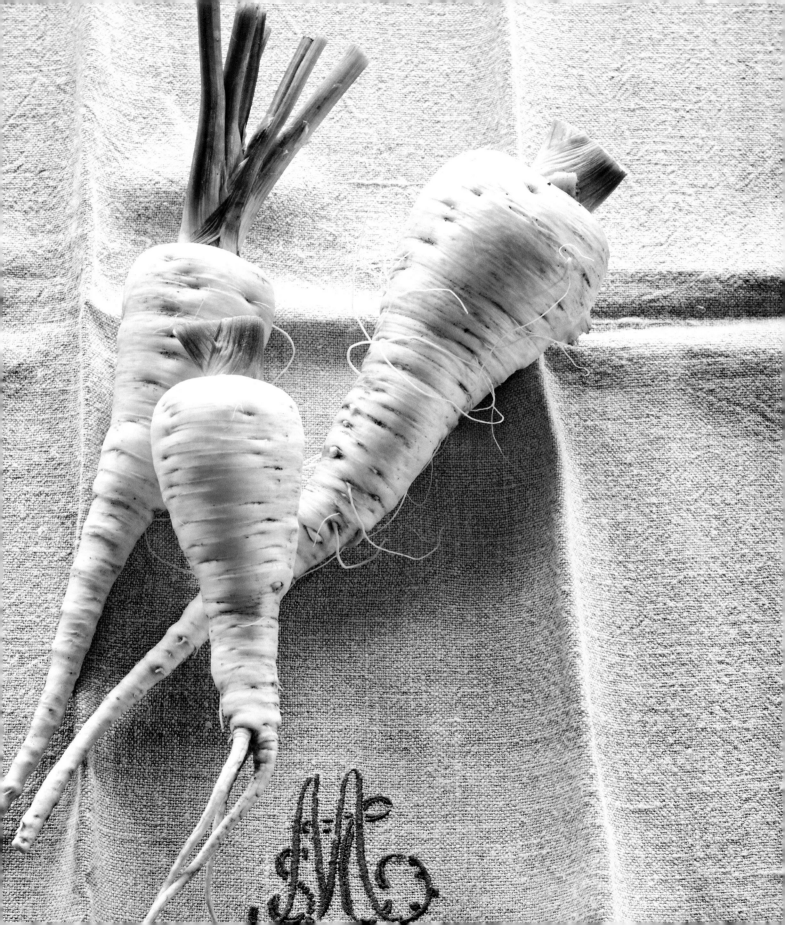

Garden Sides

Four-Root Puree

2½ pounds celeriac
(1 very large or
2 smaller), peeled and
cut into 1-inch pieces

3 pounds russet potatoes
or other starchy
potatoes, peeled and cut
into 1-inch pieces

1 large parsnip, peeled and
cut into 1-inch pieces

4 large carrots, peeled and
cut into 1-inch pieces

Kosher salt and freshly
ground white pepper

6 tablespoons unsalted
butter

This recipe is a versatile and simple way to use the root vegetables from your garden or your local market. A puree is made by peeling, boiling, and pureeing any type of root vegetable, even brassicas and squash, and flavoring it with salt, pepper, butter, and sometimes cream or milk. On occasion, I might add soft roasted garlic, an herb or two, and possibly tomato paste or stock to the recipe. Last year, we had a wonderful crop of celeriac, large flavorful parsnips, sweet carrots, and fabulous potatoes, and I put all four together with some butter, salt, and pepper, and the resulting puree was gobbled up. For dinners, purees can be served with roasts, chicken, steaks, and even fish. They add color and variety to any meal. Oftentimes I will prepare two or three, making sure each is colorful and tasty.

SERVES 10 TO 12

1. Place each vegetable in its own pot. Cover with water by 1 inch. Add 1 teaspoon salt to each pot. Bring to a boil, reduce heat, and simmer until tender: 10 to 15 minutes for celeriac and potatoes; 10 to 12 minutes for parsnip and carrots. Drain all the vegetables, reserving 1 cup of the potato cooking liquid.

2. Working in batches, puree the vegetables in a food processor, adding the potato cooking liquid to create a smooth puree. Stir in the butter until the butter melts. Season with salt and white pepper. Serve hot.

Smashed Baked Potatoes with Crème Fraîche & Caviar

6 Yukon Gold or russet potatoes, scrubbed

Kosher salt

Unsalted butter, for serving

Crème fraîche, for serving

Best-quality caviar (such as Black Diamond Ossetra) or salmon roe, for serving

Yet another favorite at my restaurant, The Bedford, is surprisingly the humble, or not so humble, smashed baked potato. Years ago, while researching the potato-growing area of northern Maine, Aroostook County, I learned that once baked in its jacket or skin, a potato should be smashed on the kitchen counter before adding your desired toppings, like butter, sour cream, crème fraîche, and caviar. Why? Smashing the roasted potato breaks the tough fibers of the cooked flesh, leaving it airy, light, and easy to eat. Of course, you must first bake the potato long enough for it to become fluffy when smashed. Then carefully slit the skin along the length of the potato and, holding it with a small cloth or potholder to prevent burning one's hand, smash it, slit-side down, quite forcibly on the counter. This might cause consternation among family or friends the first time around, but that is part of the fun! Once these are tasted, everyone present will forevermore smash their baked potatoes.

SERVES 6

1. Preheat the oven to 375°F, with a rack set in the center. Bake the potatoes on a rimmed baking sheet until darkened slightly, beginning to wrinkle, and easily pierced with the tip of a knife, 60 to 90 minutes (depending on size), flipping potatoes halfway through.

2. Working one at a time, use the tip of a knife to slit the skin along the length of each potato. Then immediately wrap the potatoes in a clean kitchen towel and smash them, slit side down, onto a countertop to break the fibers (this ensures a light, fluffy texture). Season with salt, and top generously with butter, dollops of crème fraîche, and scoops of caviar. Serve immediately.

THE MIGHTY POTATO

Potatoes are and have been a very big part of my diet.
I incorporate them into many of my menus. They are versatile,
tasty, nutritious, and very useful. Potatoes are the base for
many soups, as well as a main ingredient (like with potato-and-
buttermilk soup). Scalloped or mashed, they are among my
favorite sides, and as a filling for Big Martha's pierogi, they are
essential. I have visited the potato farmers in northern
Maine, in Aroostook County, where I learned how to harvest the
famous baking potato, and how to roast it and serve it.
Topped with butter, crème fraîche, and embellished with a
generous serving of caviar, a baked smashed potato
is one of the most popular appetizers on my menu at
The Bedford in Las Vegas.

Every spring we plant many different types of potatoes
in my garden; some of the varieties have included Russet Burbank,
Dark Red Norland, Elba, German Butterball, Chieftain, Satina,
Yukon Gem, and, of course, Yukon Gold. Potatoes are grown from
seed potatoes. We cut the seed potatoes so that each piece has
at least two eyes, leaving the smallest potatoes whole; then we dip all
the cut surfaces into ground fir bark, a natural fungicide, and
let them dry for a few days before planting. I so look forward to
the harvest when I can include the potatoes in my cooking.
My one regret is that I have yet to grow a potato large enough, dry
enough, and shapely enough to serve baked and smashed
at my own table.

Photo by Richard Phibbs, 2008

VEGETABLE COOKERY

Blanched Green Beans

So many people have a difficult time cooking the ubiquitous string bean. Here is a proven method, ensuring tender but not mushy, and still nicely crunchy, bright **green beans**. Make sure the beans are young, not discolored, and snap when bent. Trim the stem ends. Bring a large pot of water to a rolling boil, **salt** generously, and cook the green beans until they are flaccid when shaken gently with your fingers. Drain, and then immerse immediately in ice water to cool. To serve, heat ½ cup water with 2 tablespoons **unsalted butter** in a large skillet. Add the drained beans and cook until just heated through. Season with **salt** and **pepper** and a bit more butter, if you wish.

Wilted Spinach

I absolutely adore spinach. I use my homegrown spinach every day in my green juice. I fold fresh spinach leaves into my scrambled eggs or frittatas. I cream blanched chopped spinach in a simple béchamel like my mom did and use it in popovers or to accompany a roasted chicken. And if I have baby spinach leaves, I make a salad with a rich vinaigrette flavored with chopped shallots and a few crispy lardons of delicious bacon for the best simple salad ever! To cook perfect **spinach**, start with tender leaves, well washed and spun almost dry. Place the leaves in a covered saucepan and steam until wilted. Drain well, chop, and season with **butter**, **salt**, and **pepper**. That's it.

Simmered Asparagus

Of course, fresh garden **asparagus** are best when plump. Fat asparagus are my favorite, 6 to 8 inches long. With a vegetable peeler, remove the skin 2 to 3 inches from the bottom of the stem. Arrange the asparagus neatly in a deep skillet of salted boiling water, and cook until the asparagus are tender to the point of a sharp knife—they should be wobbly, but not collapse, when you hold an end and shake. Drain and chill the asparagus in ice water if to be served cold; otherwise serve hot out of the pan, bright green, with some **unsalted butter**, a few drops of fresh **lemon juice**, and **salt** and **pepper**.

Boiled Carrots

Peel and cut bright sweet **carrots** into desired pieces. The carrots can be orange, white, yellow, or dark purple. I prefer cutting carrots into quarter-turn pieces or slicing them evenly. Cook the carrots in salted boiling water until tender. Serve them hot out of the water, with **butter, salt**, and **pepper** and garnished with freshly **chopped herbs**, such as chervil or parsley, if desired.

MARTHA'S NOTE

To roll-cut carrots (as shown here), slice on a 45-degree angle, rotating a quarter turn between each slice. Slice, rotate, and slice; rolling and cutting until you're finished.

Big Martha's Mashed Potatoes

Kosher salt and freshly ground pepper

3½ pounds medium Yukon Gold potatoes (about 9)

8 ounces cream cheese, softened

1 stick (½ cup) unsalted butter, softened

½ cup heavy cream, warmed

¼ cup whole milk, warmed

One of our family's favorite vegetable dishes growing up were the delicious mashed potatoes Mom would prepare to accompany her roast pork loin, roasted chicken, and big roasted turkey on Thanksgiving. Her secrets? Idaho potatoes, peeled and boiled until fork-tender. Lots of fresh butter. A lot of cream cheese and hot milk added for creaminess. Salt and pepper, of course. It was not possible to find Yukon Golds in the Nutley Co-Op, where we shopped for all our groceries in the '40s, or in the Shop-Rite, which came to Nutley in the early '50s. But these days, I love the tenderness of Yukon Golds, and I grow a hardy crop of them in my Bedford garden. I also use both heavy cream and milk—and I use a food mill with the finest sieve to ensure creamy, smooth, and silky mashed potatoes. The best ever!

SERVES 8

1. Fill a large pot with 1 to 2 inches of water and add a pinch of salt. Set a steamer basket in the pot, making sure the water doesn't seep through the holes. Bring to a boil, then reduce to a rapid simmer. Add the whole potatoes to the basket and steam until they are tender when pierced with the tip of a paring knife, 30 to 40 minutes, depending on size. Remove from the pot and let stand until just cool enough to handle. Rub off the skins and discard. Cut the potatoes into pieces and pass through a food mill or ricer into a bowl.

2. Add the cream cheese, butter, cream, and milk to the bowl and mash with a masher. Alternatively, beat with an electric mixer. Season with salt and pepper, and beat to desired consistency. Return the mashed potatoes to the pot to keep warm until serving.

Miso Eggplant

FOR NOBU'S DEN MISO

1½ cups white miso

¾ cup sugar

¾ cup sake

¾ cup mirin

FOR THE EGGPLANT

4 Japanese eggplants (about 6 ounces each)

Extra-virgin olive oil, for frying

1 tablespoon toasted sesame seeds

Pickled ginger and plums, for serving (optional)

Nobu Matsuhisa and I became friends at his eponymous first restaurant in New York in 1994. Long a fan of Japanese cuisine, I was enchanted with Nobu and his incredibly careful, delicious, and creative interpretation of Japanese food. Nobu's early recipes were simple, influenced by his travels around the world, and each incorporated ingredients that were purely Japanese but also others that were international, such as in his yellowtail sashimi with jalapeño peppers and yuzu. I have eaten at many of Nobu's fifty or so restaurants worldwide, and Miso Cod and Miso Eggplant have been and still are my favorites. I grow many Japanese-type eggplants (such as Asian Delite, Shoya Long, and Orient Express) every summer, and I frequently serve this recipe inspired by Nobu himself, as a side dish with his Miso Cod, or as a main course by itself with rice.

SERVES 4

1. Make the den miso: Combine the miso and sugar in a medium heavy-bottomed saucepan. Add the sake and mirin, whisking to combine. Bring to a simmer over low heat and cook, stirring frequently, until the sugar is dissolved and the color begins to darken, 30 to 45 minutes. Remove from the heat. (You should have about 2½ cups; reserve 1 cup and set aside the rest for another use.)

2. Preheat the broiler. Line one baking sheet with paper towels and a second sheet with foil; set aside.

3. Make the eggplant: Halve the eggplants lengthwise. Using the tip of a sharp knife, score the flesh in a crosshatch pattern. In a large heavy-bottomed saucepan, heat 2 inches of oil to 360°F. Working in batches, fry the eggplants, skin-side up, 1 minute. Turn and fry until tender, 30 to 90 seconds more. Transfer to the paper-towel-lined sheet; let drain.

4. Transfer the eggplants, skin-side down, to the foil-lined baking sheet. With a spoon, spread each half with a generous 1 tablespoon den miso. Broil until the sauce begins to caramelize, 30 seconds to a few minutes, depending on the strength of your broiler. Sprinkle with the sesame seeds and serve with the pickled ginger and plums, if desired.

Nobu Matsuhisa and me, making sushi for a May 1997 story in my magazine; we've been friends ever since.

Street Corn

8 ears of corn

Vegetable oil, for
the grill grates

2/3 cup finely crumbled
Cotija cheese

2/3 cup mayonnaise
(I like Hellmann's)

Cayenne pepper, for
sprinkling

Chopped cilantro, for
sprinkling

Chopped fried dried
peppers, for sprinkling
(I like Cruschi,
but it's optional)

Lime wedges,
for serving

When I was growing up, corn was one of our family's favorite summer side dishes, off the cob, steamed, buttered, and paired with baby lima beans—all homegrown, tender, and utterly delicious. Later, when I summered in East Hampton, at my beautiful home on Lily Pond Lane, we couldn't wait for the corn from local farms. The first Butter and Sugar ears would arrive in July, with kernels alternating between white and pale yellow. We would always get a baker's dozen (thirteen ears), shuck the husks into the compost bin, and boil the cobs in salted, sugared water until the sweet smell of cooked corn permeated the kitchen. The steaming platter of corn on the cob would be served with sticks of salted butter, salt, and maybe chile pepper. It wasn't until I went to Mexico City and ate elote every day that corn took on an entirely new meaning for me. Corn became the meal. Two or three ears, amazingly flavored, was all I wanted with a fresh margarita in a salt-rimmed glass. I now grow corn here on my Bedford farm just for my own version of street corn. Enjoy!

MAKES 8 EARS OF CORN

1. Peel back the corn husks, leaving them attached at the base of the ears. Remove and discard the silk; pull the husks back over the corn. Place the ears in a large bowl or pot and cover with cold water. Let soak for 10 minutes. Drain the corn.

2. Preheat the grill to medium-high and lightly oil the grates. Arrange the ears on the grill. Cover and cook, turning occasionally using tongs, until the husks are slightly charred and the corn is tender, 15 to 20 minutes.

Remove the ears from the grill. Holding the bottom of the hot ears with a towel, peel back the husks and tie with cooking twine.

3. Place the Cotija on a plate. Brush a thin layer of mayonnaise on the corn, then roll the corn across the cheese. Sprinkle the corn with cayenne, chopped cilantro, and chopped fried dried peppers, as desired. Serve with lime wedges.

WESTON TOWN FAIR

The town of Weston, Connecticut, held a fair each summer
in the Norfield Grange Hall on Good Hill Road, and there were
several classes of vegetables to enter. I was gardening at
the time, in Westport on my six-acre "farmette," and I created
a wonderful display of ten vegetables. I included several
varieties of each vegetable, causing a bit of consternation
among the judges, who thought I had not followed
instructions. I argued that eggplants were eggplants, and tomatoes
were tomatoes, and that each combined should count as an
eggplant or a tomato. I won the argument as well as the Best in
Show ribbon for my display, and other blue ribbons for
individual varieties. It was my nature then, as well as now, not to do
the ordinary, but to elaborate on the ordinary and create, as
best as I could, the extraordinary. I continue to garden, and finding
seeds around the world to grow the unique and the unusual
has become my passion. Just a year ago, we started a very large
vegetable garden composed of raised beds. The beds are
filled with a mixture of homemade compost, professionally
composted soil, various nutrients, and manures. It has transformed
my growing of edible, nutritious vegetables exponentially,
and what I have grown has been amazing and delicious. Many of
the vegetables and fruits used in the photos and recipes in
this book were grown in the new raised beds and in my orchard
and berry patches.

Photo courtesy of author, 1970s

Onion Rings

2 cups instant flour, such as Wondra

1 teaspoon kosher salt

½ teaspoon baking powder

¼ teaspoon freshly ground white pepper

1 cup beer, preferably lager or pilsner

2 tablespoons ice water

Peanut oil, for frying

2 medium Vidalia onions, cut crosswise into ½-inch-thick slices, separated into rings

Fine sea salt, for sprinkling

Lemon wedges, for serving

You will find very little deep-fried food in this book. Twenty years ago when I was building my dream kitchen at the farm, I installed a magnificent Jade gas range that has a salamander broiler, a griddle, six burners, a grill, three ovens, and a large deep fryer. I have never used the deep fryer, however, preferring to fry tempura or potatoes or onions in a heavy, tin-lined copper tempura pan. As a result, I never have to deal with large quantities of frying oil. I have always been a big fan of Riad Nasr and Lee Hanson, the two founding chefs of Balthazar restaurant in New York City. It was there I first tasted their magnificent onion rings and learned the recipe that I immediately added to my collection. The combination of very finely milled flour added to ice water and beer makes a crunchy light batter that coats each ring perfectly. You will always make this recipe once you have tasted these Vidalia rings.

SERVES 6

1. Whisk together 1 cup instant flour, the kosher salt, baking powder, and white pepper in a bowl. Whisk in the beer and ice water until combined. Place the remaining cup instant flour in a shallow dish.

2. Preheat the oven to 200°F. Top a rimmed baking sheet with a wire rack and place in the oven on the middle rack. Heat 3 inches of oil to 375°F in a heavy, deep pot over medium-high.

3. Dredge the onions in the instant flour, turning to coat; tap off the excess. Working in batches (about 8 at a time), dip the floured onions in the batter with a fork, shaking off the excess. Carefully add them to the hot oil and cook until golden brown, 2 to 3 minutes. Adjust the heat as necessary to keep the oil at a steady temperature. Transfer them to paper towels to drain and sprinkle with fine sea salt. Transfer to the baking sheet to keep warm while cooking the remaining onions. Serve hot with lemon wedges.

Scalloped Potatoes

3 pounds Yukon Gold potatoes, peeled, and thinly sliced

2 cups milk

1½ cups heavy cream

1 garlic clove

3 tablespoons unsalted butter, softened

1 tablespoon kosher salt

½ teaspoon freshly ground white pepper

Pinch of cayenne pepper

4 ounces Gruyère cheese, coarsely grated (about 1 cup)

Whole nutmeg

Thyme sprigs, for serving

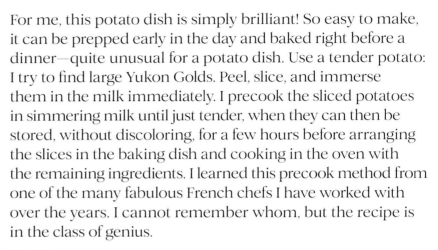

For me, this potato dish is simply brilliant! So easy to make, it can be prepped early in the day and baked right before a dinner—quite unusual for a potato dish. Use a tender potato: I try to find large Yukon Golds. Peel, slice, and immerse them in the milk immediately. I precook the sliced potatoes in simmering milk until just tender, when they can then be stored, without discoloring, for a few hours before arranging the slices in the baking dish and cooking in the oven with the remaining ingredients. I learned this precook method from one of the many fabulous French chefs I have worked with over the years. I cannot remember whom, but the recipe is in the class of genius.

SERVES 8

1. Preheat the oven to 325°F, with a rack set in the lower third of the oven. Combine the sliced potatoes and the milk in a large saucepan over high heat. Bring to a boil and immediately reduce the heat to low; cover and simmer until the potatoes are just tender, about 3 minutes.

2. Place a colander over a large bowl and drain the potatoes, reserving the milk. Add the cream to the milk and stir to combine.

3. Rub a 3½-quart oval baking dish with the garlic and 1 tablespoon butter. Arrange the sliced potatoes in the baking dish; season with the salt, white pepper, and cayenne. Dot with the remaining butter and pour the reserved cooking milk and cream over the potatoes. Sprinkle the cheese over the top.

4. Grate the nutmeg over the top and garnish with thyme. Transfer the baking dish to the oven and bake until the cheese becomes deep golden brown and the milk has reduced and thickened, 80 to 90 minutes. Remove from the oven and serve immediately, with additional thyme sprigs.

Persian Rice
(*Tahdig*)

4 cups basmati rice, rinsed until water runs clear, and drained

Kosher salt

¼ teaspoon saffron

3 tablespoons hot water (160°F to 180°F)

7 tablespoons unsalted butter

When Homa Dashtaki, the lovely founder of the White Moustache yogurt, came on my Roku show, she demonstrated the proper techniques for making tahdig. Since our lesson, I have had great success with this simple recipe. I use my own saffron, which I have been growing since 2020, planting the corms in late summer and harvesting the blooms in fall. Each purple bloom has three stigmas, which must be carefully plucked, dried, and preserved for cooking.

SERVES 8

1. Place the rinsed and drained rice in a bowl, and cover it with cold water. Add 3 tablespoons salt and stir to combine. Let stand for 1 hour. Drain the rice and rinse.

2. Bring a large wide pot of water to a boil. Generously salt the water, then add the rice. Cook until the rice has just a bit of bite in the center, 5 to 8 minutes. Drain it through a fine-mesh sieve. Rinse with cool water and drain again.

3. In a small bowl, steep the saffron in the hot water until the liquid is bright orange, about 5 minutes.

4. Heat the same pot over medium-high heat until it is dry. Add 6 tablespoons butter and cook until melted (the bottom of the pot should be covered with a healthy layer of butter). Wrap the lid of the pot with a clean kitchen towel. Spoon the par-cooked rice into the pot, forming a mound. Use the handle of the spoon to poke 6 to 8 holes into the rice, and add a pat of the remaining butter to each hole. Drizzle the rice evenly with the saffron liquid. Cover the pot and cook over medium-high until you hear a distinct sizzling sound (this jump-starts the formation of the crust).

5. Reduce the heat to low, and cook until the rice is tender and fluffy, 20 to 30 minutes, turning the pot a quarter turn about every 6 minutes to ensure even browning. Remove from the heat, set on a wet towel (this will help get the tahdig out), and let stand for 5 minutes.

6. Run an offset spatula around the edges of the rice to loosen it. Place a large plate or platter, upside down, over the pot. Use oven mitts to grab the pot handles and platter at the same time, and flip the pot over so the platter is on the bottom. Use the handle of a spoon to gently tap the bottom of the pot to separate the rice from pot. Carefully lift off the pot. If any pieces of crust have stuck to the pan, use an offset spatula to remove them and place atop the rice. Serve immediately.

Desserts

Blood-Orange Granita

10 blood oranges

I am so fortunate to have a grove of potted citrus trees on my farm in Bedford. These trees, most of them about nine or ten feet tall, potted in large planters, and fed weekly, stay indoors during the winter months and outdoors in the sunshine the rest of the year. I have been collecting all my favorite types of citrus for fifteen years or so, and I am thrilled at the amount and variety of delicious fruits I harvest every year. Blood oranges, homegrown like this, are extra-special, with their very sweet, dark-red flesh and blood-red juice. Variations on this one-ingredient dessert can be made from the juice of oranges, grapefruits, sweetened lemons, sweetened limes, or even pomegranates or apples. Oh, I almost forgot, sweetened espresso coffee! I have experimented with this preparation often and have liked this one the best so far. Serve granita on its own or with a dollop of whipped cream, a cookie, or even a piece of cake.

SERVES ABOUT 4

MARTHA'S NOTE

A shallow baking dish is ideal for quick freezing and easy scraping of the ice crystals as they form.

Juice the blood oranges. (You should have about 2 cups.) Pour the juice into a baking dish and place it in the freezer. Freeze, for at least 2 hours, scraping every 30 minutes or so with a fork to fluff. Spoon into small chilled glasses and serve.

Fudgy Brownies with Hot Fudge Sauce

1 stick (½ cup) unsalted butter, cut into large pieces

6 ounces bittersweet chocolate, chopped

1½ cups sugar

3 large eggs

¼ cup unsweetened Dutch-process cocoa powder

½ teaspoon kosher salt

½ cup plus 2 tablespoons unbleached all-purpose flour

Vanilla ice cream, for serving

Hot Fudge Sauce (recipe follows), for serving

I had been searching for the fudgiest, richest brownies for a long time, and these are the ones I like best. The combination of bittersweet chocolate and Dutch-process cocoa creates a dark brownie with a crunchy yet smooth top that cuts nicely into squares and behaves perfectly as a base for vanilla ice cream with real hot fudge. Simple to prepare, easy to bake ahead, this is a favorite yet unexpected dessert at a dinner party. Guests just love the old-fashioned nature of this combination.

MAKES NINE 2½-INCH BROWNIES

1. Preheat the oven to 350°F. Line an 8-inch square baking pan with parchment, leaving a slight overhang on all sides. Melt the butter and chocolate in a double boiler or a heatproof bowl set over a pot of simmering water, stirring until smooth. Remove from the heat and whisk in the sugar. Whisk in the eggs, one at a time, until combined. Whisk in the cocoa and salt. Fold in the flour until combined.

2. Pour the batter into the prepared pan. Bake until set and a cake tester inserted into the center comes out with moist crumbs, 35 to 40 minutes. Let cool slightly in the pan, about 15 minutes. Lift the brownies from the pan using the parchment. Remove the parchment and transfer to a wire rack. Let cool completely. Cut into 9 squares. Serve with ice cream and hot fudge. (Brownies can be stored in an airtight container at room temperature up to 2 days.)

Hot Fudge Sauce

MAKES ABOUT 2 CUPS

Combine ½ cup **sugar**, ¼ cup **unsweetened Dutch-process cocoa powder** (such as Valrhona), ¾ cup **heavy cream**, ¾ cup **light corn syrup**, ½ teaspoon kosher **salt**, and 3 ounces chopped **semi-sweet chocolate** in a medium saucepan. Bring to a boil over medium-high heat, whisking frequently. Continue to cook, whisking frequently, until the bubbles slow and the mixture is thick and glossy, 4 to 7 minutes. Remove from heat and stir in 2 tablespoons **unsalted butter** and 1 teaspoon **pure vanilla extract**. Keep warm until ready to use. (Store refrigerated up to 3 weeks. Reheat over low before serving.)

Brown-Sugar
Angel Food Cake

1¼ cups sifted cake flour
(not self–rising)

1½ cups packed light brown
sugar

14 large egg whites,
at room temperature

1½ teaspoons cream of
tartar

Pinch of kosher salt

2 teaspoons finely grated
lemon zest

8 ounces crème fraîche,
for serving

Strawberries,
for serving

My sister Kathy, fourth in the lineup of six siblings in the Kostyra family, always asked for and received an angel food cake for her birthday. Mom would save up egg whites prior to her special day, January 16, and whip up a light and airy cake that she served with homemade strawberry jam (since fresh strawberries were out of season) and softly whipped heavy cream. When I started baking seriously for my catering business, The Uncatered Affair, I experimented with many different recipes, even with a boxed version, of this perennial favorite. I playfully substituted brown sugar for white and was delighted with the result, which you'll find here. Of course, you must follow the preparation, baking, and cooling instructions, and obtain an angel food cake pan. Serve with seasonal fruit (strawberries or peaches are delicious) and with crème fraîche or ice cream.

SERVES 10

1. Preheat the oven to 350°F. In a medium bowl, stir together the flour and ¾ cup brown sugar. Sift twice.

2. Put the egg whites into the bowl of a stand mixer fitted with the whisk attachment. Beat on medium speed until foamy. Add the cream of tartar and salt. Raise the speed to high and beat until soft peaks form. Sprinkle half of the remaining ¾ cup brown sugar over the egg white mixture and beat until combined. Sprinkle the remaining brown sugar over the egg white mixture and beat until stiff, glossy peaks form.

3. Transfer the egg white mixture to a large bowl. Fold in the flour mixture in 3 batches, folding in the lemon zest with the last addition.

4. Spoon the batter into an ungreased 10-inch tube pan (not nonstick) with a removable bottom. Run a knife through the batter to eliminate any air pockets. Bake until the cake is golden and springs back when lightly touched, about 45 minutes.

5. Invert the pan onto its legs or over a narrow-neck bottle; let cool for 1 hour. Reinvert and run a knife around the sides and tube to loosen; remove the sides. Run a long knife along the bottom of the cake; remove from the tube. Place the cake on a platter and serve with crème fraîche and strawberries.

ALL ABOUT FAMILY

THIS IS THE ONLY FAMILY PHOTO of the Kostyra family, which includes our mother and father (Big Martha and Edward) and all six children (*from left*) Frank, me, Eric, Kathryn, Baby Laura, and George. It was a professional photo, taken in our home at 86 Elm Place in Nutley, New Jersey. I wish I had more of these family portraits, as it's very interesting to see how a family grows and changes over the years. I especially love the holiday cards some of my friends send year after year, posing with pets and in different locations. In fact, I have saved many of those cards because, for me, they are illustrative history.

My mother had her six children over a period of eighteen years, starting with Eric, then me, Frank, Kathy, George, and Laura. We lived in a three-bedroom house, with one bathroom and one powder room. Somehow we were always well groomed, clean, and well dressed, and we were always on time for school, sports, and work. Mom did the shopping, most of the cooking, and the cleanup, and even returned to teaching when Laura went to kindergarten at age five. She was an accomplished and creative cook, and maybe even a better baker. The six of us children never had what you'd call junk food, but we did have scrumptious homemade sweet treats—cookies, pies, and cakes—and when a birthday would roll around, the one celebrating their special day would have their favorite "cake."

For my sister Kathy, it was that delightfully airy angel food cake; brother George's "cake" was sour cherry pie. For Dad, it would be yellow layers with orange-lemon filling and rich dark chocolate frosting. My own favorite was Lady Baltimore cake—which is a tall white layer cake with a chewy fruit and nut filling and a spectacular cloud of seven-minute frosting.

My mother had a charming little cookbook, published by General Foods in 1933, called *All About Home Baking,* where she found a number of delicious cakes. She always enjoyed trying classics as well as newer recipes. I followed suit. Later, I loved baking the cakes in both volumes of *Mastering the Art of French Cooking,* by Julia Child, Simone Beck, and Louisette Bertholle; from Maida Heatter's books; and from *The Silver Palate Cookbook.* I experimented with other cakes that I discovered through travel or work—including the showstopping Cipriani Classic Meringue Cake that follows—but I've always loved returning to the basics, like my Apple Crumb Pie (page 278). Simple or sophisticated, baking is a sweet tradition that never gets old.

Photo courtesy of author, 1950s

Cipriani Classic Meringue Cake

FOR CAKE ASSEMBLY

300 grams Pastry Cream (Crema Pasticcera; recipe follows)

 1 liter heavy cream

50 grams confectioners' sugar

 4 layers Sponge Cake (Pan di Spagna; recipe follows)

FOR THE MERINGUE

150 grams egg whites, at room temperature

300 grams sugar

Juice of ½ lemon

MARTHA'S NOTE

You will need the very freshest farm eggs, the best heavy cream, a superb vanilla bean, and a small propane torch for toasting the meringue.

I first tasted this extraordinary cake in Venice at the original Harry's Bar, opened by Giuseppe Cipriani, Sr., in 1931. When the Cipriani restaurant came to New York City in the '80s, I again sampled this incredible confection and became determined to learn the secret of its preparation. Well, it took until 2023, when I visited Casa Cipriani in downtown Manhattan, on the East River in the old ferry terminal, where I filmed a delightful young Italian baker preparing this cake for our TV show. It's not uncomplicated to make and does require quite a bit of time, but the result is spectacular and definitely worth it! It is and always will be my favorite cake.

SERVES 10

1. Whip the pastry cream, heavy cream, and confectioners' sugar until very stiff. Set aside.

2. Assemble the cake: Put the bottom layer of the cake on a baking sheet and spread one third of the filling over it, leaving a ½-inch margin on the cake. Top it with another layer of cake and another third of the filling. Repeat, then add the top layer of cake.

3. Make the meringue: Be sure the egg whites are at room temperature. In a medium bowl, beat the egg whites and the sugar until frothy. Add the lemon juice. Beat the meringue until it is very thick and glossy.

4. Spread the meringue thickly over the cake with a knife or a spatula. Gently press the spatula down on the meringue and lift it straight up to form decorative peaks. Using a kitchen torch, toast the meringue until golden brown. (Alternatively, toast the cake in a 500°F oven for 2 to 3 minutes. Watch it carefully and remove the cake from the oven as soon as it looks good.) Carefully slide the cake onto a platter and chill until you're ready to serve.

continued

265 grams milk

100 grams heavy cream

105 grams sugar

Zest of ½ a lemon

1 vanilla bean, split lengthwise and scraped

3 large egg yolks

45 grams unbleached all-purpose flour

Pastry Cream (*Crema Pasticcera*)

MAKES ABOUT 2 CUPS

1. Combine the milk, cream, half of the sugar, the lemon zest, and vanilla bean in a heavy-bottomed saucepan and bring to a boil. Remove from heat and discard the lemon zest and vanilla bean.

2. In a bowl, whisk the egg yolks with the remaining sugar. Whisk in the flour until the mixture is smooth. Gradually whisk the hot milk into the yolk mixture and pour the mixture back into the saucepan.

Cook the custard over medium-low heat, stirring constantly, until it thickens and boils again. Continue to cook over low heat for 3 to 4 minutes, stirring frequently.

3. Remove from the heat and let the custard cool, stirring frequently to keep a skin from forming. Press plastic wrap directly onto the surface of the cream to further prevent a skin from forming. Refrigerate the custard for at least 2 hours before using it. (You can make the pastry cream up to 24 hours in advance.)

Unsalted butter, softened, for pan

200 grams unbleached all-purpose flour, plus more for dusting

6 large eggs, at room temperature

140 grams egg yolks

180 grams sugar (a rounded cup)

Sponge Cake (*Pan di Spagna*)

MAKES 1 SPONGE CAKE

1. Preheat the oven to 350°F. Butter and flour a 9-inch (23 cm) cake pan or springform pan.

2. Beat the eggs and egg yolks with the sugar until the mixture is very thick and pale yellow.

3. Sift the flour onto the egg mixture and gently fold in. Do not beat the batter; cut straight to the bottom of the bowl with a spatula and lift the batter up and over the flour. When the flour is incorporated, scrape the batter into the prepared pan and bake until the cake is golden and a cake tester inserted in the center comes out dry, 25 to 28 minutes.

4. Let the cake cool briefly on a rack. Remove it from the pan and let it cool completely. Using a serrated knife with a long blade, slice it horizontally into 4 layers. Immediately wrap the layers in plastic wrap until ready to use them. If you don't plan to use the cake the same day, you can freeze it, well wrapped, indefinitely.

Upside-Down Lemon Meringue Pie

FOR THE CRUST

Unsalted butter, softened, for pie dish

4 large egg whites, at room temperature

¼ teaspoon cream of tartar

1 cup sugar

FOR THE FILLING

8 large egg yolks, at room temperature

1 cup sugar

1 tablespoon plus 1 teaspoon finely grated lemon zest (from 2 lemons)

¼ cup plus 2 tablespoons fresh lemon juice (from 2 lemons)

1 cup cold heavy cream

Whipped Cream (page 288), for serving

MARTHA'S NOTE

I sometimes make a very large version if I am having lots of guests for dinner, and at the restaurant, we make individual pies, generously sized for one.

In 2014, one of the magazine food editors, Laura Rege, suggested we feature her grandmother's most divine Lemon Angel Pie, also known as Upside-Down Lemon Meringue. I had been served such a pie in Jacksonville, Florida, and had been searching for a recipe. I now make this dessert often, and we feature it on the menu of my restaurant in Las Vegas. It is popular because it is so very delicious: Silky-smooth egg whites, beaten with lots of sugar, are formed into a "crust" in an ovenproof glass or porcelain pie dish, then filled with lemon curd and topped with softly whipped cream.

SERVES 8

1. Make the crust: Preheat the oven to 300°F with the rack in the center. Lightly brush a 9-inch pie dish with butter. In the bowl of a stand mixer fitted with the whisk attachment, beat together the egg whites and 1 tablespoon cold water on high speed until foamy, about 30 seconds. Add the cream of tartar and continue to beat until soft peaks form, about 1 minute. Gradually add the sugar and beat until thick, glossy peaks form, about 5 minutes.

2. Transfer the egg-white mixture to the prepared pie dish; spread along the bottom and up the sides to form a crust. (Don't spread past the rim of the dish.) Bake the meringue crust until crisp and light golden on outside, about 40 minutes. Turn off the heat and let cool in the oven 1 hour, then transfer to a wire rack to cool completely.

3. Make the filling: Whisk the egg yolks in a medium saucepan (off heat) until thickened and pale yellow, 1 to 2 minutes. Whisk in the sugar and lemon zest and juice. Place over medium heat and cook, stirring constantly with a wooden spoon, until the mixture is very thick, about 10 minutes. Transfer to a large bowl. Cover with plastic wrap, pressing it directly onto the surface of the curd. Refrigerate until chilled, for at least 1 hour and up to 1 day.

4. Whisk the chilled curd until smooth. In the bowl of a stand mixer fitted with the whisk attachment, whip the cream on high until soft peaks form, about 1 minute. Working in batches, gently fold the whipped cream into the curd. Fill the meringue crust with the lightened curd, smoothing the top with an offset spatula. Refrigerate, loosely covered, for at least 8 hours and up to 1 day. Top with whipped cream and serve.

Strawberry Shortcake

FOR THE BISCUITS

- 4 cups unbleached all-purpose flour, plus more for dusting
- ½ cup granulated sugar
- 2 tablespoons baking powder
- 1 teaspoon kosher salt
- 1½ sticks (¾ cup) cold unsalted butter, cut into pieces
- 2 cups cold heavy cream
- 1 large egg, lightly beaten
  Coarse sanding sugar

FOR THE STRAWBERRIES

- 3 pints strawberries, hulled
- 1 tablespoon fresh lemon juice
- ⅓ cup granulated sugar
  Whipped Cream (page 288)

There are three essential ingredients for the very best strawberry shortcake: flaky, plump biscuits; red, ripe, delicious strawberries; and freshly whipped cream. The biscuits in this recipe are just right, enriched with heavy cream, rolled a bit thick, and baked with a sanding sugar surface that adds crunchiness and sweetness to the dessert. Split the biscuits crosswise, spoon some macerated berries on the bottom half, dollop with a generous helping of whipped cream and some more strawberries, then top with the upper half. Some unhulled berries will look pretty on the plate, and if they are from your own berry patch, all the better.

SERVES 8

1. Make the biscuits: Preheat the oven to 400°F. Place the flour, granulated sugar, baking powder, and salt in the bowl of a food processor; pulse a few times to combine. Add the butter and pulse until the mixture resembles coarse crumbs with some pea-size pieces remaining. Add the cream and pulse until the dough just comes together (it will be sticky).

2. Transfer to a lightly floured work surface and, with floured fingers, pat the dough to a 1¼-inch thickness. Cut out rounds with a 2½-inch cutter, cutting as close together as possible.

3. Place the biscuits on an unlined baking sheet, about 1½ inches apart. Brush the tops of the biscuits with the beaten egg and sprinkle with sanding sugar. Bake until the biscuits are golden, 20 to 25 minutes, rotating the sheet halfway through.

4. Make the strawberries: While the biscuits bake, slice the strawberries in half (or quarters, if large). In a medium bowl, toss the strawberries with the lemon juice and sugar. Let the mixture macerate for 30 minutes.

5. After baking the biscuits, transfer them to a wire rack to cool for 15 minutes; then split them in half horizontally with a serrated knife. Spoon the whipped cream and strawberries on the bottom biscuits and serve them with the top halves.

Rum Butter Bundt Cake

- 2 sticks (1 cup) unsalted butter, softened, plus more for pan
- 3 cups unbleached all-purpose flour, plus more for pan
- 1 teaspoon baking powder
- 1 teaspoon baking soda
- 1 teaspoon kosher salt
- 2 cups sugar
- 4 large eggs
- 2 teaspoons pure vanilla extract
- 2 tablespoons rum
  Grated zest of 1 lemon
- 1 cup buttermilk

continued

For years, our company has been producing extraordinary Martha brand baking pans with Nordic Ware, a wonderful manufacturer in Minnesota. We created turkey-shaped baking pans (I use them for cornbread or cranberry molds at Thanksgiving) and swirl Bundt pans in a variety of patterns. Personally, I prefer more complex patterns in cast aluminum over the traditional Bundt pan. Preparation of the pan prior to pouring in the batter and baking the cake is essential. I use a soft bristle brush to get softened unsalted butter into every nook and cranny of the pan. A very, very light dusting of flour can also aid in releasing any cake from this type of pan. The beauty of this rum butter cake is twofold: the batter itself, enriched with vanilla and buttermilk, and, almost more important, the rum, sugar, and butter glaze that is brushed on the cake when it is removed from the oven. The texture of this cake is like a fine French pound cake, a quatre quart, but the flavor is quite different—and the glaze is a game-changer.

SERVES 10 TO 12

1. Make the cake: Preheat the oven to 325°F, with a rack set in the center. Butter and lightly flour a 10- to 15-cup Bundt pan. In a large bowl, sift together the flour, baking powder, baking soda, and salt.

2. In the bowl of a stand mixer fitted with the paddle attachment, cream the butter with the sugar on medium-high speed until light and fluffy, about 3 minutes. Add the eggs one at a time, beating well after each egg. Add the vanilla, rum, and zest. Reduce speed to medium-low and add the flour mixture in two additions, alternating with the buttermilk. Spoon the batter into the prepared pan, smoothing the top with an offset spatula.

continued

FOR THE GLAZE

- 1 **stick (½ cup) unsalted butter**
- ¼ **cup rum**
- 1 **cup sugar**
- 1 **tablespoon pure vanilla extract**
- **Whipped Cream (page 288), for serving (optional)**

3. Bake until a cake tester inserted into the center of the cake comes out clean, about 1 hour.

4. Meanwhile, make the glaze: In a small saucepan, cook the butter over medium heat until boiling. Remove from the heat and carefully add the rum; the mixture will bubble. When the bubbling subsides, stir in the sugar and vanilla. Return to medium-low heat and cook, stirring, until the sugar dissolves, about 1 minute. Remove from the heat.

5. When the cake is done, transfer the pan to a wire rack set on a baking sheet or a piece of parchment, and pierce the cake 30 times with a bamboo skewer. Brush the surface with half the glaze and allow to cool for 1 hour. Turn the cake out onto the wire rack and brush with the remaining glaze. Let cool before serving with whipped cream, if desired.

Apple Brioche Bread Pudding with Crème Anglaise

Unsalted butter,
for pan

9 large eggs

3 cups whole milk

2 cups heavy cream

¾ cup granulated sugar

1 tablespoon pure vanilla
extract

¾ teaspoon ground
cinnamon

½ teaspoon kosher salt

¼ teaspoon freshly grated
nutmeg

1½ large loaves day-old
brioche (1½ pounds
total), cut into 1-inch
cubes

½ cup golden raisins

½ cup dark raisins

Juice of 1 orange

½ cup cognac

3 pounds apples (6 to
8 mixed apples,
such as Empire, Macoun,
and McIntosh)

Juice of 1 lemon (about
3 tablespoons)

3 tablespoons coarse
sanding sugar

Crème Anglaise
(recipe follows)

I often make large amounts of something special for everyone who works on the farm. This might be a very large frittata if I have a plethora of eggs and lots of farm-grown vegetables. It might be a couple of large berry crisps or cobblers when we have just-picked bowls of beautiful blueberries or gooseberries. And when we are picking the apples from the dozens of bountiful old apple trees on the farm, it could very well be an apple brioche bread pudding, studded with raisins, currants, or dried apricots, and flavored with a custard of heavy cream, eggs, and a splash or two of cognac, Grand Marnier, or even rum. Since I often bake brioche, I keep a stash of this tasty bread in my freezer. We are also fortunate to be able to buy brioche in New York City at Balthazar Bakery or in LA at République Café & Bakery, and I keep that in the freezer also. Bake your bread pudding in a porcelain baking dish, well buttered, taking care to toss the bread cubes in the custard mix just long enough to wet them but not long enough to allow them to become soggy. I often add the grated rind of oranges or lemons, some pure vanilla extract, and some fresh orange juice for additional flavor. The apples should be peeled, cored, and cut into same-size wedges. If additional dried fruits are to be used, such as raisins or apricots, soak them in orange juice or liqueur to plump and soften. Bake just until the custard has set and the top of the sugar-sprinkled cubes of brioche are tinged a golden brown. Serve warm or at room temperature with crème anglaise, whipped cream, or just as is.

SERVES 12

1. Preheat the oven to 325°F. Lightly butter a 3½-quart baking dish.

2. In a medium bowl, whisk together the eggs, milk, cream, granulated sugar, vanilla, cinnamon, salt, and nutmeg. In a large bowl, pour the egg mixture over the bread, gently folding to combine. Let it stand for about 30 minutes.

continued

3. Meanwhile, place both the golden and dark raisins in a small bowl. Pour the orange juice over the raisins. In a small saucepan, heat the cognac until warmed. Pour over the raisins and let sit until the egg mixture is ready, allowing the raisins to plump. (This step can be done the night before.)

4. Peel, core, and cut the apples into ¼-inch-thick wedges and transfer to a large bowl. Toss them with the lemon juice. Fold the apples and plumped raisins, with the cognac-orange mixture, into the brioche mixture and transfer to the buttered dish with a slotted spoon. Pour any remaining liquid over the top and sprinkle with coarse sanding sugar.

5. Transfer to the oven and bake until the apples are tender, the center is set, and the liquid is absorbed, about 1 hour 30 minutes. Transfer to a wire rack to cool for 10 to 20 minutes before serving with crème anglaise.

MARTHA'S NOTE

If the topping is browning and the pudding is not yet set, tent with parchment-lined foil to cover it.

Crème Anglaise
MAKES ABOUT 2 CUPS

Combine 1¼ cups **milk** and ¾ cup **heavy cream** in a saucepan. Split ½ **vanilla bean** lengthwise and scrape it into the milk mixture; add the pod. Bring to a simmer over medium heat. Whisk together ½ cup **cognac**, 4 large **egg yolks**, 3 tablespoons **sugar**, and a pinch of kosher **salt** in a bowl. While whisking, slowly add about half the hot milk mixture to the yolk mixture to temper, then pour the mixture back into the pan with the remaining milk mixture. Cook over medium heat, stirring constantly, until the mixture is thick enough to coat the back of the spoon, about 5 minutes. Strain through a fine-mesh sieve into a bowl, pressing with a flexible spatula to extract as much liquid as possible; discard the solids. Cover with plastic wrap and refrigerate until chilled, for at least 2 hours and up to 2 days.

MAKING BREAD

AFTER I LEFT MY JOB ON WALL STREET, I thought long and hard about what I really wanted my next career move to be. First I opened a small independent shop, the Market Basket, on the Post Road in Westport. I called upon a group of friends who were excellent cooks to make some special food items for the store, which also sold products for the home and kitchen. I utilized that shop as a prototype for a much larger one, also called the Market Basket. This was a store within a store in the Common Market, a wonderful clothing store in the center of downtown Westport.

My shop attracted a lot of attention and regular customers, including Paul Newman, Joanne Woodward, and even Robert Redford! I bought wonderful foodstuffs from local suppliers who were cooking at home—scones, cakes, cookies, breads, quiches, and entrées of all sorts. In this photo, I am shown with breads and pastas and other products that I made at my home for the shop. We also catered and did a huge takeout business. I wanted the fact that everything was homemade to be 100 percent evident, and I think we accomplished that.

Photo by Joseph Kugliesky, 1989

Lemon Sugar Cookies

3 cups unbleached
all-purpose flour

1 teaspoon baking soda

¼ teaspoon table salt

1¾ cups granulated sugar

¼ cup packed light brown
sugar

1 tablespoon finely grated
lemon zest plus
1 tablespoon fresh lemon
juice (from 1 lemon)

2 sticks (1 cup) unsalted
butter, softened

2 large eggs

Sanding sugar, for
sprinkling

This is a very delicious, chewy, crunchy lemon-flavored treat that is great for the cookie jar, lovely to serve with tea, and wonderful for lemon ice-cream cookie sandwiches (yes, I can make lemon ice cream!). True lemon flavor is one of my favorite things, and this cookie provides that perfectly. I like to make them oversize, one per serving. Be sure to use the best unsalted butter, fresh lemon zest, and fresh lemon juice and, to achieve the light golden-brown color of the ideal cookie, bake on parchment-lined cookie sheets.

MAKES ABOUT TWENTY 3½-INCH COOKIES

1. Preheat the oven to 350°F. In a large bowl, whisk together the flour, baking soda, and salt.

2. Put the granulated sugar, brown sugar, and lemon zest in the bowl of a stand mixer fitted with the paddle attachment. Mix on medium speed for 30 seconds. Add the butter and mix until pale and fluffy, about 1 minute. Mix in the eggs, one at a time, then add the lemon juice. Reduce the speed and gradually add the flour mixture, mixing until just combined.

3. Scoop the dough using a 2-inch ice cream scoop, and space the cookies 2 inches apart on parchment-lined baking sheets. Flatten the cookies slightly with a spatula. Sprinkle the tops with sanding sugar, then lightly brush with a wet pastry brush and sprinkle with more sanding sugar.

4. Bake the cookies until golden, about 15 minutes, rotating the pans halfway through. Transfer the baking sheets to wire racks to cool for 5 minutes. Transfer the cookies to the racks using a spatula and let cool completely. (Cookies can be stored in an airtight container at room temperature up to 3 days.)

Alexis's Chocolate-Chip Cookies

3½ cups unbleached all-purpose flour

2 teaspoons baking soda

1½ teaspoons table salt

4 sticks (2 cups) unsalted butter, softened

3 cups packed light brown sugar

1 cup granulated sugar

4 large eggs

2 teaspoons pure vanilla extract

1 (12-ounce) bag (2 cups) best-quality chocolate chips, such as Guittard or Valrhona

Flaky sea salt, such as Maldon, for sprinkling

When I started my catering business, I collected as many delicious cookie recipes as I could. Chocolate-chip cookies were so varied in texture, taste, appearance—some were plump and chewy, others dry and crumbly, others thin and crispy. My daughter developed this recipe, which became an instant favorite and remains so to this day. The combination of brown sugar, white sugar, eggs, and butter yields a crispy yet chewy and exceedingly flavorful cookie that spreads quite thin when baked on ungreased heavy-duty baking pans. The perfect cookie is large, thin, and generously studded with chocolate chips and has concentric circles on its surface.

MAKES THIRTY 4-INCH COOKIES

1. Preheat the oven to 375°F. Whisk together the flour, baking soda, and salt in a large bowl.

2. In the bowl of a stand mixer fitted with the paddle attachment, cream the butter until light and fluffy. Add both sugars and beat until smooth. Beat in the eggs and vanilla. Slowly beat the flour mixture into the egg mixture. Fold in the chocolate chips.

3. Scoop the dough, using a ¼ cup scoop, and place onto ungreased, unlined baking sheets, spacing at least 2 inches apart to allow for spreading.

4. Bake the cookies until golden, 10 to 12 minutes, rotating the pans halfway through. Transfer the baking sheets to wire racks and sprinkle Maldon salt on top of the cookies. After 5 minutes, transfer the cookies to the wire racks and allow them to cool before serving.

Alexis at our little Middlefield cottage in the Berkshires, circa 1970.

Brown-Butter Shortbread Cookies

15 tablespoons unsalted butter, cut into pieces

2 teaspoons pure vanilla extract

2 cups unbleached all-purpose flour, plus more for dusting

½ cup granulated sugar

1 teaspoon baking powder

½ teaspoon table salt

¼ teaspoon ground cardamom

⅓ cup coarse sanding sugar

A few years ago, the brown-butter craze began, and suddenly brown butter was turning up in cakes, brownies, and cookies. Statistically, the interest in brown butter grows each year, as restaurants and recipes incorporate this nutty, darkish flavoring in more and more foods. At *Martha Stewart Living*, we were ahead of the phenomenon, presenting my mother's recipe for potato pierogi with brown butter in 1997. (My mom used brown butter as a flavoring for pierogi as well as for bland vegetables like cauliflower for as long as I can remember, but I do not recall if she ever incorporated it into a recipe for a cake or cookie.) For me, brown butter was a game-changer when it was used in our shortbread cookie recipe. The crumbly, dry, sandy shortbread dough blossomed with its addition. When you make these cookies, you will find out for yourself. And, by the way, try serving Stilton cheese with these cookies during cocktail hour—so utterly delicious.

MAKES ABOUT 40 COOKIES

1. Melt the butter in a small saucepan over medium heat. Continue to cook, stirring constantly, until deep golden brown, 10 to 11 minutes. Immediately pour the butter into a large bowl and let cool to room temperature, about 10 minutes. Stir in the vanilla.

2. In a medium bowl, whisk together the flour, granulated sugar, baking powder, salt, and cardamom. Gradually stir the dry ingredients into the brown-butter mixture. Roll out the dough to a generous ¼-inch-thick square on parchment or Silpat. Sprinkle the dough with the sanding sugar and lightly roll it into the dough. Dip 1½-inch fluted cutters into the flour and punch out the cookies. Transfer the cookies to parchment-lined baking sheets and refrigerate until chilled, for at least 30 minutes and up to overnight.

3. Preheat the oven to 350°F. Bake the cookies until light brown and firm, 15 to 17 minutes. Let cool completely on the baking sheets on wire racks before serving.

Puff Pastry, Two Ways

1 cup sugar, for sprinkling

1 pound 4 ounces homemade Puff Pastry (page 290) or store-bought puff pastry (such as Lecoq Cuisine)

Vegetable oil cooking spray, for racks

4 cups Whipped Cream (page 288)

About 4 cups golden raspberries (from three 6-ounce containers)

Puff pastry, or pâte feuilletée as the French call it, is quite a versatile dough. I love to use it for Napoleons, tarts, palmiers, Pithiviers, pigs in a blanket, vol-au-vents, chicken potpies, and, of course, filet de boeuf en croûte (beef Wellington). I have always enjoyed the regal Napoleon, here kept simple and light, with whipped cream and golden raspberries. The sheets of pastry can be baked early in the day, and filled and layered a few hours prior to serving.

Raspberry Napoleon

SERVES 8 TO 10

1. Preheat the oven to 375°F, with one rack in top third and one in center. Sprinkle the work surface with some of the sugar. Place the pastry on top and roll to about a 12-inch square, about ⅛-inch thick, continually sprinkling with additional sugar to prevent sticking. Using a sharp knife or pastry cutter, trim the edges. Cut into three 4-by-12-inch rectangles. Lightly spray two baking sheets with water and place the pastry on them (2 sheets on one and 1 sheet on the other). Refrigerate for 30 minutes.

2. Dock the rectangles all over with the tines of a fork. Coat two wire cooling racks with vegetable spray and place a rack over each tray (be sure that the feet of the rack do not touch the pastry). Bake, rotating the pans top to bottom and back to front halfway through, until the pastry rises and touches the rack, 15 to 20 minutes. Carefully remove the wire racks and continue to bake until golden brown and cooked through, about 10 minutes more. Immediately run an offset spatula under the pastry to release them from the pans; then transfer the pastry to wire racks to cool completely.

3. Fill a pastry bag fitted with a large star tip, such as Ateco #825, with the whipped cream. Pipe even rows of cream onto one piece of pastry. Top the piped stars with the berries. To help secure the layers, pipe a line of cream in the center, on top of the berries. Repeat this process on a second piece of pastry. Place this second layer on top of the first. Top with a final piece of pastry. Refrigerate, loosely covered, for at least 1 hour and up to 1 day. Use a serrated knife and a sawing motion to cut into pieces just before serving.

¾ **cup sugar, for sprinkling**

1 **pound homemade Puff Pastry (page 290; about ⅓ of recipe) or store-bought puff pastry (such as Lecoq Cuisine)**

Palmiers

It was in Paris, when I was just seventeen, that I first discovered these flaky, heavenly treats. One day I picked out a large palmier, and I was hooked for life. I vowed to bake them when I returned to the States, not knowing how time-consuming it was to make pâte feuilletée, the puff pastry. I did eventually master the technique, and my passion grew so large that I even purchased a professional sheeter with which to form this delicate, many-layered laminated dough. It's very important to follow the directions carefully to create an acceptable palmier. When you do, make a lot and freeze them, baked or unbaked. You will be happy you did.

MAKES 36 PALMIERS

1. Sprinkle a work surface with the sugar. Place the puff pastry on top and roll to an 8-by-26-inch rectangle approximately ⅛-inch thick, continually sprinkling with additional sugar to prevent the dough from sticking.

2. Working quickly but gently, roll each long end to the center of the pastry, making sure to roll tightly and evenly. Freeze the rolled log for 20 minutes, until very firm but not frozen. Slice crosswise into ⅜-inch slices. Roll over each palmier with a rolling pin to lightly flatten, then sprinkle the center of each with more sugar. Place palmiers 2 inches apart on water-sprayed baking sheets. Freeze for at least 1 hour.

3. Preheat the oven to 450°F. Bake the palmiers 4 to 6 minutes, until golden on the underside. Flip with a spatula, pressing down to flatten if the palmiers seem to be unrolling. Bake 2 to 4 minutes more, watching carefully, until golden and crisp. Transfer the palmiers to a cooling rack and cool completely.

MARTHA'S NOTE

I find black steel sheet pans excellent for puff pastry, as they conduct heat very well, resulting in even browning.

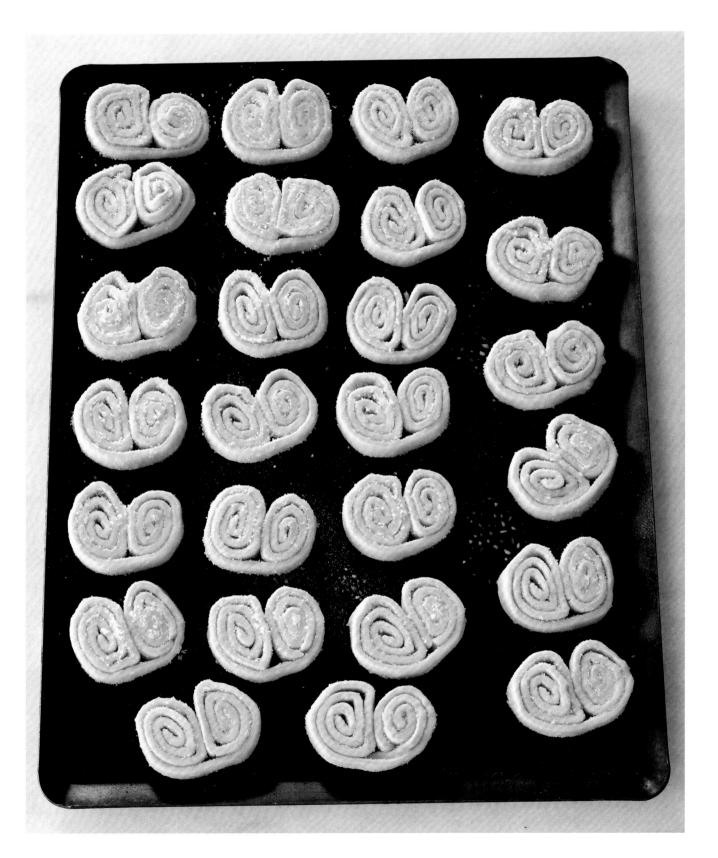

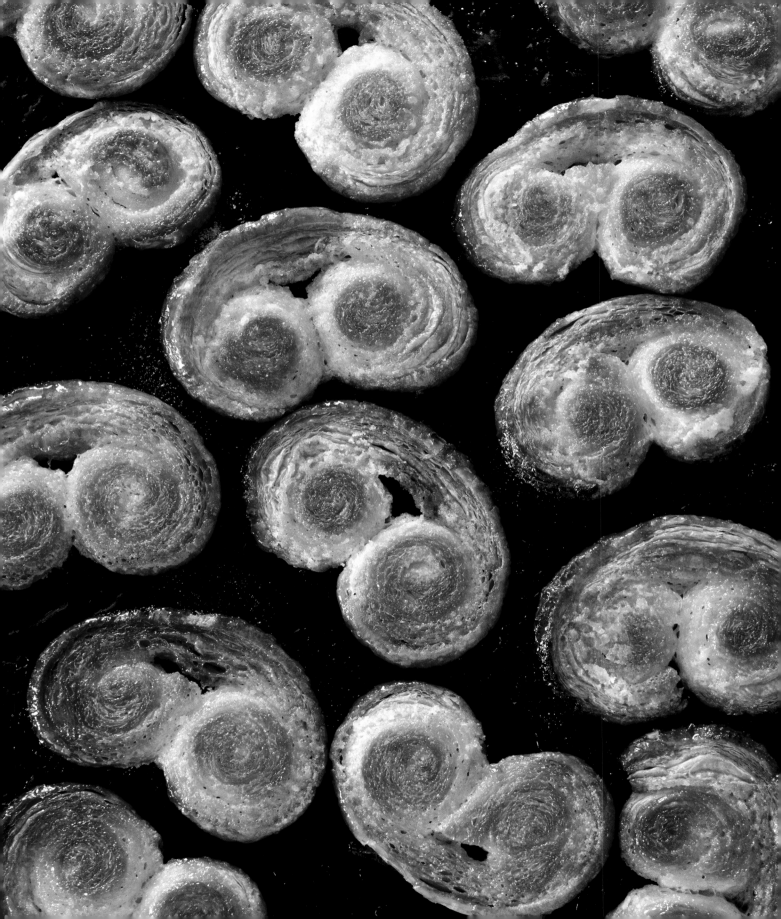

MODELING DAYS

After my first year at Barnard College, I was sent by my modeling agency to Paris to do the winter fashion shows in the summertime. I had never been to that magnificent city; I was not fluent in French, although I could converse very simply; and it was my very first trip abroad. I was put up in a charming hotel on the Left Bank, Hôtel Scandinavia, just below Luxembourg Palace. The neighborhood was lovely, old-fashioned, and full of wonderful boulangeries, pâtisseries, fromageries, and charcuteries. This was prior to the supermarket type of food store we are now so accustomed to. I shopped carefully, wanting to taste everything, to discover the best of the best of each and every baguette, croissant, pastry, cheese, jambon, and beurre.

I had a productive, instructive, and very good trip. But I realized that to be a successful model would take more time than I was willing to spend as a seventeen-year-old student. I returned to New York, wiser and a bit more sophisticated, and continued modeling part-time while I went to college. I had long, dark blond hair, clear skin, and a good figure—natural but not sexy or exciting like supermodel Veruschka, or sophisticated like Penelope Tree, or perky like Twiggy. Nevertheless, my rate increased to fifty dollars an hour and I worked as often as my schedule allowed, appearing in *Glamour* and *Mademoiselle,* modeling for Francesco Scavullo, Richard Avedon, Henri Dauman, Horn & Griner, and even William Silano. Modeling prepared me very well for my future television work and for posing for thousands of pictures for magazines, mine included!

Photos courtesy of author

Unsalted butter,
for the baking dish

FOR THE FILLING

3 pounds peaches, halved
lengthwise, pitted, and cut
into ½-inch-thick wedges

2 pints raspberries

¼ cup granulated sugar

2 tablespoons cornstarch

4½ teaspoons fresh lemon
juice

FOR THE CRUMBLE

¾ cup unbleached
all-purpose flour

½ cup old-fashioned oats

½ cup granulated sugar

¼ cup packed dark brown
sugar

½ teaspoon ground
cinnamon

Large pinch of kosher salt

6 tablespoons unsalted
butter, chilled and cut into
pieces

Peach and Raspberry Crumble

In August 2005, we did a wonderful story in *MSL* distinguishing the characteristics of crumbles, crisps, cobblers, buckles, grunts, slumps, and pandowdies. It turned out that there are significant differences and yet no set rules, because many people call crisps crumbles, crumbles crisps, slumps grunts, and buckles cobblers. We tried to research with as much care as possible, and the following three desserts are as close to fitting their names as we think they can be. That said, forgive us if you disagree. My peaches and raspberries ripen at about the same time here at the farm, and that is when I concentrate on fruit desserts using them. This crumble has a textured sugary topping of oats, brown sugar, flour, and cinnamon. The fruit below the topping features a simple mix of sugar, cornstarch, and fresh lemon juice. Of course, this traditional topping can be used on many other fruits—pears, apples, plums, gooseberries, whatever your preference. No matter what filling you choose, you will love a good crumble.

SERVES 4

1. Preheat the oven to 375°F. Butter a 2½-quart baking dish. Line a rimmed baking sheet with parchment and top with a wire rack.

2. Make the filling: Stir together the peaches, raspberries, granulated sugar, cornstarch, and lemon juice in a large bowl. Transfer to the prepared dish.

3. Make the crumble: Combine the flour, oats, both sugars, cinnamon, and salt in a medium bowl. Cut in the butter with a pastry blender, or your fingers, until the mixture is crumbly.

4. Sprinkle the crumble mixture over the fruit. Transfer the crumble to the prepared baking sheet and bake until the top is browned and juices are bubbling, 40 to 50 minutes. Let cool on a wire rack, about 30 minutes, before serving.

Plum Cobbler

Unsalted butter,
for the baking dish

FOR THE FILLING

3 pounds plums or
pluots, halved length-
wise, pitted, and cut into
½-inch-thick wedges

¼ cup granulated sugar

2 tablespoons cornstarch

1 tablespoon fresh lemon
juice

½ teaspoon kosher salt

FOR THE BISCUITS

1½ cups unbleached
all-purpose flour

3 tablespoons granulated
sugar

1½ teaspoons baking
powder

¼ teaspoon baking soda

¾ teaspoon kosher salt

6 tablespoons unsalted
butter, chilled and cut
into pieces

⅓ cup low-fat buttermilk

⅓ cup heavy cream, plus
more for brushing

Coarse sanding sugar, for
sprinkling

Over the years, there has been an extraordinary evolution in the world of plums and plum varieties grown for the market. Growing up, I knew the Blue Damson plum, the Stanley Italian prune plum, and a red sweet-sour plum. Now there are Santa Rosa plums, lemon plums, Italian sugar plums, Burgundy plums, AU Rosa plums, Satsuma plums, and about thirty-five hybrids, including pluots, plumcots, and apriums. Each type is certainly worth trying, and many would be superb in any of my crisps, cobblers, or crumbles. For this recipe, we used a red-skinned, yellow-fleshed Japanese pluot. The biscuit topping is extremely light, fluffy, and tender, and the sanding sugar crust makes for a wonderful final touch atop the dessert.

SERVES 8

1. Preheat the oven to 375°F. Butter a 2½-quart baking dish. Line a rimmed baking sheet with parchment and top with a wire rack.

2. Make the filling: Stir together the plums, granulated sugar, cornstarch, lemon juice, and salt in a large bowl. Transfer the plum mixture to the prepared dish.

3. Make the biscuits: In a large bowl, whisk together the flour, granulated sugar, baking powder, baking soda, and salt. Using a pastry blender or your fingers, cut in the butter to form clumps no larger than small peas. Stir in the buttermilk and cream until a soft, sticky dough forms.

4. Using a scoop, form 8 biscuits. Top the fruit with the biscuits, spacing evenly. Brush the biscuit tops with cream and sprinkle with sanding sugar. Transfer to the prepared baking sheet and bake until golden brown and bubbling in the center, about 1 hour 15 minutes. Let cool on a wire rack, 30 minutes, before serving.

Blueberry Crisp

6 tablespoons unsalted butter, chilled and cut into pieces, plus more for the dish

¾ cup unbleached all-purpose flour

½ cup granulated sugar

¼ cup packed dark brown sugar

½ teaspoon ground cinnamon

Large pinch of kosher salt

5 cups blueberries

My research tells me that a crisp is a baked fruit dessert with a topping of butter, sugar, flour, and spice. My favorite version is made with a generous layer of fresh New Jersey highbush blueberries beneath a thick topping. This superb dessert can be made as one large dish or many smaller ones for individual servings. Large or small, you'll know it's done when the fruit filling is bubbling in the center. Topped with vanilla ice cream, or whipped cream, it's an easy and delicious crowd-pleaser.

SERVES 4

1. Preheat the oven to 375°F. Butter a 1½-quart baking dish. Line a rimmed baking sheet with parchment and top with a wire rack.

2. Combine the flour, both sugars, cinnamon, and salt in a large bowl. Cut in the butter with a pastry blender, or your fingers, until the mixture is crumbly.

3. Place the blueberries in the prepared dish. Sprinkle the crumble mixture over the blueberries. Transfer the dish to the prepared baking sheet and bake until the top is browned and juices are bubbling, 30 to 40 minutes. Let cool on a wire rack, about 30 minutes, before serving.

MARTHA'S NOTE

When I bake fruit desserts, I line my rimmed baking sheet with parchment and then top it with a wire rack. Any fruit juices will drip onto the parchment and cleanup is easy and efficient.

Buttermilk Sorbet

1 cup sugar

2 cups buttermilk

½ teaspoon grated lemon zest plus 3 tablespoons lemon juice (from 1 lemon)

1 tablespoon corn syrup

1 pinch of kosher salt

No dessert is easier to pull together than this one. Of course, it is important to have an ice cream maker; there are many on the market, but look for a large electric model that is not complicated to use. In terms of ingredients, I use an organic full-fat buttermilk, freshly grated lemon zest, and fresh lemon juice. Meyer lemons add a unique and wonderful flavor to this sweet-sour icy dessert. I have made yogurt sorbet, sour cream sorbet, and crème fraîche sorbet and find this buttermilk version to be the best.

MAKES 6 CUPS

1. In a small saucepan, bring the sugar and 1 cup water to a boil, then remove from the heat. Refrigerate for at least 1 hour or until chilled.

2. In a large bowl, whisk together the buttermilk, lemon juice, corn syrup, and salt. Slowly add the chilled syrup and whisk to combine. Stir in the lemon zest. Freeze in an ice cream maker, following the manufacturer's instructions. When freezing is complete, transfer the sorbet to an airtight container and place in the freezer for at least 1 hour. Serve as desired. (Sorbet will keep, frozen, up to 2 weeks.)

Applesauce Tart

- 1 cup Pink Applesauce (recipe follows)
- ¼ cup granulated sugar
- 2 tablespoons white rum

  Unbleached all-purpose flour, for dusting
- 1 disk (½ recipe) Pâte Brisée (page 288), chilled
- 2¼ pounds apples (4 to 5), peeled, cored, and sliced about ¼ inch thick (5½ to 6 cups)
- 2 tablespoons fresh lemon juice

  Pinch of kosher salt
- ¼ cup coarse sanding sugar

This is the kind of tart you wish was served at a sit-down dinner, or at the diner. The crust, buttery and flaky, is topped with pinkish applesauce, which is then adorned in concentric circles with thin, peeled slices of sweet-tart apples. These in turn are sprinkled with sanding sugar and baked in a hot oven until the fruit is tender, the crust crispy and brown, and the sanding sugar slightly caramelized. To make the best version, first you must perfect your pâte brisée. Once you feel comfortable with that crust, you can prepare any number of pies and tarts. Just remember my golden rule for pie crust, however: "Make it cold, bake it hot."

SERVES 10

1. Heat the applesauce, granulated sugar, and rum in a small saucepan over medium-low, stirring to dissolve the sugar. Set aside to cool completely.

2. On a lightly floured surface, roll out the dough to a ⅛-inch-thick round. Fit into an 11- or 12-inch round fluted tart pan with a removable bottom, pressing the dough up to the rim of pan. Freeze for 15 minutes.

3. In a large bowl, toss the apples with the lemon juice and salt.

4. Preheat the oven to 400°F. Spread the applesauce mixture evenly into the chilled tart. Starting from the center and working outward, shingle the apples in tight concentric circles over the applesauce. Sprinkle with the sanding sugar.

5. Bake until the apples are tender, 45 to 60 minutes. Transfer to a wire rack to cool. Unmold and serve warm or at room temperature.

Pink Applesauce

MAKES ABOUT 2½ CUPS

Core and quarter 3 pounds (6 to 8) **apples**, such as McIntosh and Empire; do not peel. Place in a medium saucepan. Add the juice of 1 **lemon** and a pinch of kosher **salt**. Cover and cook over low heat, stirring occasionally, until the apples break down to a sauce-like consistency. Remove from heat, uncover, and let stand until the apples cool slightly. Using tongs or chopsticks, discard the skins. Mash the apples for a chunky consistency. Use immediately, or store in an airtight container in the refrigerator up to 1 week.

Tarte au Fromage

FOR THE CRUST

Unbleached all-purpose flour, for dusting

1 disk (½ recipe) Pâte Brisée (page 288), chilled

FOR THE FILLING

1⅓ cups sugar

1 tablespoon plus 1 teaspoon unbleached all-purpose flour

2⅓ cups (18 ounces) farmer cheese, at room temperature

⅔ cup crème fraîche, at room temperature

1 large egg yolk plus 4 large egg whites, at room temperature

Heaping ¼ teaspoon kosher salt

1½ teaspoons pure vanilla extract

1 tablespoon plus 1 teaspoon unsalted butter, melted

When I wrote my first *Pies and Tarts* cookbook, in the '80s, I had yet to taste a tarte au fromage. We published our recipe in *MSL* in 2012, and I prepared this dessert on my television show *Martha Bakes* shortly thereafter. It has since become a staple in our repertoire and a favorite on our tables. Surprisingly, it does remind me of my buttermilk pie with its lemony custardiness, but the similarity ends there. The combination of fresh farmer cheese and crème fraîche results in a light filling that pairs extremely well with the flakiness of the buttery, well-baked pâte brisée crust. It is easily mistaken for a classic cheesecake, but it is, rather, a very flavorful, light, vanilla-infused cheese tart. Once you try it, you will make it again and again!

SERVES 10

1. Make the crust: On a lightly floured work surface, roll out the dough to a 12-inch round. Fit the dough into a 9½-by 2-inch round fluted tart pan with a removable bottom, pressing the dough up to the rim of pan. Freeze until firm, about 15 minutes.

2. Preheat the oven to 375°F with a rack in the center. Place the pan on a baking sheet. Line the pastry with parchment, pressing it into the edges, and fill it with beans or pie weights. Bake until the sides are golden, about 30 minutes. Remove the paper and weights and continue baking until the crust is light golden brown, about 10 minutes more. Transfer to a wire rack to cool.

3. Make the filling: Lower the oven to 350°F. In a medium bowl, whisk together 1 cup sugar and the flour. In another medium bowl, whisk together the cheese, crème fraîche, egg yolk, salt, vanilla, and butter. Add the sugar mixture and stir to combine.

4. In the bowl of a stand mixer fitted with the whisk attachment, beat the egg whites on medium until foamy. Raise the speed to medium-high and gradually add the remaining ⅓ cup sugar. Beat until medium glossy peaks form, about 4 minutes. Fold half the egg whites into the cheese mixture; then fold in the remaining egg whites.

5. Add the filling to the cooled tart shell and bake until just set (it should wobble when very lightly shaken), 45 to 55 minutes. Let cool, undisturbed, on a wire rack for 1 hour before unmolding. The tart is best served slightly warm but can also be served at room temperature.

Cranberry Tart

FOR THE CRUST

Unbleached all-purpose flour, for dusting

1 disk (½ recipe) Pâte Brisée (page 288), chilled

FOR THE FILLING

2 (¼-ounce) envelopes unflavored gelatin

6 cups fresh cranberries

1¾ to 2 cups sugar, to taste

1 cup red currant jelly

2 tablespoons cognac

Whipped Cream (page 288), for serving (optional)

This is a simple, delicious, and very pretty dessert that requires a baked pâte brisée tart shell and a cooked cranberry filling. If you are entertaining, this can be made the day before and kept chilled. It slices into lovely wedges and is complemented nicely with dollops of whipped cream. Every Thanksgiving, I create a list of pies to make for the farm staff. For the past three years, this cranberry tart has been the most popular, along with the Pumpkin Pie with Phyllo Crust (page 276). I like to use fresh cranberries, if possible, but frozen are also acceptable. The pâte brisée can be made in batches and frozen in flat disks for pie making anytime. I often make four or five batches at a time for the freezer. No excuses for lack of time when your family needs or wants a homemade pie or tart.

SERVES 10

1. Make the crust: On a lightly floured work surface, roll the dough into a 13-inch round. With a dry pastry brush, sweep off any excess flour. Fit the dough into a 10-inch round fluted tart pan with a removable bottom, pressing the dough up to the rim of pan. Pierce the bottom of the tart shell all over with a fork. Freeze until firm, about 15 minutes.

2. Preheat the oven to 375°F. Uncover and line the tart shell with parchment, pressing it into the edges, and fill with beans, rice, or pie weights. Bake until the sides are set and golden, about 20 minutes. Remove the weights and parchment and continue baking until the bottom of the crust is dry and golden, 15 to 20 minutes. Remove from the oven and let cool completely on a wire rack.

3. Make the filling: Sprinkle the gelatin over ½ cup cold water in a small bowl, and let stand until softened, about 5 minutes. Combine the cranberries, sugar, jelly, and cognac in a saucepan, and cook over low heat for 12 to 15 minutes. (Do not overcook, or the mixture will become too watery; the cranberries should be soft but not bursting.) Remove from the heat and let cool slightly. Stir in the softened gelatin and let cool completely. Pour the cranberry filling into the tart shell and chill for at least 1 hour before unmolding and serving with whipped cream, if desired.

Pumpkin Pie
with Phyllo Crust

¾ cup sugar

1 teaspoon Chinese
five-spice powder

8 sheets frozen
phyllo dough (each
approximately 13
by 18 inches), thawed

1 stick (½ cup) unsalted
butter, melted

3 large eggs, at room
temperature

2½ cups homemade
pumpkin puree, or
2 (15-ounce) cans pure
pumpkin puree

1 (12-ounce) can
evaporated milk

⅓ cup pure maple syrup

1 vanilla bean, halved
lengthwise and scraped

3 tablespoons unbleached
all-purpose flour

¾ teaspoon kosher salt

Whipped Cream
(page 288), for serving
(optional)

I am indeed a traditionalist when it comes to celebrating holidays—asparagus and lamb at Easter, turkey with stuffing and mashed potatoes at Thanksgiving, and roast beef and bûche de Noël at Christmas. But within every tradition, there is room for a twist, a surprise. Developed for a Thanksgiving *MSL* issue by food editor Greg Lofts, this silky-smooth pumpkin pie baked in a phyllo crust is just that sort of innovation—a break with tradition that results in exclamations of pleasure and even awe. I have always enjoyed working with phyllo, tissue-paper-thin sheets of translucent dough layered with lots of melted butter. For this pie, the crust is formed first, prebaked, then filled with a delicately flavored pumpkin custard. Bake until the crust is a nutty brown and the filling is set. Serve it with dollops of softly whipped cream.

SERVES 6 TO 8

1. Preheat the oven to 400°F. Stir together ¼ cup sugar and ½ teaspoon five-spice powder. Brush 1 sheet of phyllo with butter (as you work, keep the remaining phyllo covered with a kitchen towel); sprinkle evenly with 1½ teaspoons sugar mixture.

2. Starting at one short end, fold the phyllo in half to enclose the butter and sugar mixture; brush the top with more butter. Transfer to a 9-inch springform pan, buttered-side down, gently pressing into the bottom and sides.

3. Repeat with the remaining phyllo, butter, and sugar mixture, arranging in overlapping layers to completely and evenly cover the bottom and sides of the pan.

4. Bake until the crust is golden, 15 to 18 minutes. Transfer the pan to a wire rack and let cool completely. Leave the oven on. (The baked cooled crust can be wrapped and stored at room temperature up to 1 day.)

5. In a large bowl, whisk together the eggs, pumpkin, milk, syrup, vanilla seeds, flour, salt, and remaining ½ cup sugar and ½ teaspoon five-spice powder until smooth. Pour the mixture into the crust and bake for 20 minutes.

6. Reduce the oven to 350°F and continue baking until the custard is just set in the center, 40 to 50 minutes more. Transfer the pan to a wire rack and let cool completely. Release the sides of the pan, and serve with whipped cream, if desired.

Apple Crumb Pie

FOR THE CRUMB TOPPING

- 1⅓ cups unbleached all-purpose flour
- 1 cup sugar
- ¾ teaspoon ground cinnamon
- ¾ teaspoon kosher salt
- 2 sticks (1 cup) unsalted butter, chilled and cut into pieces

FOR THE PIE

- Unbleached all-purpose flour, for dusting
- 1 recipe Pâte Brisée (page 288), formed into a large disk and chilled
- 4 to 5 pounds mixed apples, peeled and sliced into ½-inch wedges (about 12 cups)
- Juice of 1 large lemon (3 to 4 tablespoons)
- 1 large egg, lightly whisked
- 1 tablespoon heavy cream
- ¾ cup sugar

I have made many different versions of apple pies and tarts over the years: mile-high double-crust pie, bottom-crust crostata, applesauce tart, puff-pastry apple tart, brown-butter apple pie. Lately, I have been baking this pie a lot, having discovered that the pâte brisée bottom crust stays crispy for two days, the apples cook perfectly, and the crumb topping remains a bit crispy! I frequently use a mix of my farm apples for a delicious result—some apples cook more slowly and remain a bit firm while others soften elegantly, filling in all the spaces around the firmer slices. An egg wash helps the crimped pastry edge darken nicely.

SERVES 8 TO 10

1. Make the crumb topping: Whisk together the flour, sugar, cinnamon, and salt in a large bowl. Cut in the butter with a pastry blender, or your fingers, until the texture reaches a consistency of coarse meal. Press some of the mixture together to create small clumps. Set aside.

2. Make the pie: Preheat the oven to 400°F. On a lightly floured surface, roll out the dough into a ⅛-inch-thick round. Fit it into a 12-inch round, 2-inch deep pie dish. Trim the edges to 1 inch. Fold them under and crimp as desired. Freeze until firm, about 15 minutes.

3. Meanwhile, toss the apples with 2 tablespoons lemon juice in a large bowl. In a small bowl, whisk together the egg and cream to make an egg wash.

4. Add 4 cups apples to the pie dish. Sprinkle with ¼ cup sugar. Add 4 cups more apples and ¼ cup sugar, followed by the remaining 4 cups apples and ¼ cup sugar. Drizzle with the remaining lemon juice. Sprinkle 3 cups topping generously over the apples (freeze extra for another pie or a crumble). Brush the crimped edge with the egg wash.

5. Bake the pie for 1 hour 30 minutes, until golden brown and bubbling. Let cool at least 3 hours before serving.

MARTHA, THE AUTHOR

Creating a cookbook is a very complex process and one that takes a long time to complete. This one hundredth book started many years ago when I was first collecting and developing and testing recipes to cook and to ultimately share. My process, simplified, for publishing a cookbook is as follows: Write an outline and enumerate the recipes to be included. After the editorial approval, hire a photographer, food and prop stylists and assistants, and an art director. Photograph the entire book, including cover options. Lay out all the pages with the best photos, leaving blank spots for the text. Once the agreed-upon design is set, fill in all the blanks: Write page by page, chronologically if possible.

This is the way I personally write or create a book like this. Writing to each designed and photographed page works best for me. Every photo tells me the story because it was planned to do that, and the photographer knows that from the beginning of the project. So does the stylist and the art director and anyone working on the individual photos. The writing is done by me, in the quiet of my own home. In this photo I was still using a typewriter—remember those? Now, of course, my text is written by email to my editor, Susanne. The text is then placed in the appropriate spots of the designed pages, and before too long a book has been created. Voilà!

Photo courtesy of author, 1980s

Rhubarb Lattice Tart

Vegetable spray,
for the pan

½ cup all-purpose flour,
plus more for dusting

1 recipe Pâte Brisée
(page 288), chilled

6 cups chopped rhubarb
(about 1¾ pounds)

1½ cups sugar

Juice of 1 lemon
(about 3 tablespoons)

1 large egg yolk

1 tablespoon heavy cream

I have enjoyed cooking, stewing, baking, and freezing rhubarb ever since I was a child in Nutley, New Jersey, pulling stalks from giant plants in my father's garden. Mom stewed rhubarb with a modicum of sugar, and we ate it for dessert, making faces at the sourness of this venerated vegetable masquerading as a fruit. The best rhubarb is pale, tender, and naturally sweet, grown under clay cloches or baskets in faraway places like France or Belgium. Locally, choose the reddest or pinkest rhubarb with crisp, slender stalks. Cut it into 1-inch pieces, macerating it with sugar before using, if possible. A rectangular tart like this with a geometric lattice crust permits you to cut very neat square portions. Serve with whipped cream or ice cream for perfection.

MAKE ONE 8-BY-11-INCH TART

1. Preheat the oven to 375°F. Coat an 8-by-11-inch tart pan with vegetable spray. On a lightly floured surface, roll out one half of the dough for the bottom crust. Fit into the prepared tart pan, pressing the dough up to the rim of the pan. With your thumb, clean the edge of excess pastry.

2. Place the rhubarb in a bowl and toss with the flour, sugar, and lemon juice. Spoon the rhubarb into the tart shell and place in the refrigerator to chill while preparing the lattice.

3. Roll out the remaining half of dough and cut into ½-inch strips with a zigzag cutter. Remove the tart shell from the refrigerator. Weave the strips together over the filling, pressing the edges to seal.

4. In a small bowl, whisk together the egg yolk and cream. Brush the lattice with the egg wash. Place the tart on a parchment-lined baking sheet, and bake until the pastry is golden brown and the juices in the center of the tart are bubbling, 50 to 65 minutes. Transfer to a wire rack to cool, at least 1 hour, before serving.

My Basic Pantry

BASIC RECIPES

Homemade Beef Stock

MAKES 3½ QUARTS

- 4 pounds beef bones, such as knuckles and shins
- 2 pounds short ribs or oxtail (optional)
- 3 tablespoons sunflower or other neutral-tasting oil
- 2 tablespoons tomato paste
- 2 onions, unpeeled and quartered
- 2 celery stalks, each cut into thirds
- 2 carrots, peeled and cut into 2-inch pieces
- 4 garlic cloves, unpeeled and crushed
- 1 cup water or red wine
- 6 flat-leaf parsley sprigs
- 4 thyme sprigs
- 2 dried bay leaves
- 2 teaspoons whole black peppercorns
- 1 tablespoon kosher salt

1. Preheat the oven to 400°F. Arrange the bones and short ribs (if using) in a single layer in a large, heavy roasting pan. Drizzle with oil and turn to coat. Roast, turning once and stirring often for even browning, until beginning to brown, about 45 minutes. Remove from the oven, add the tomato paste, and stir to combine. Cook on the stovetop over medium heat for about 30 seconds (to let it brown a little, which cooks out some of the acidity and intensifies the sweetness of the paste), then add the onions, celery, carrots, and garlic, stirring well. Return to the oven and roast until the vegetables are browned and tender and the bones are deeply browned, about 40 minutes.

2. Transfer the bones and vegetables to a large stockpot, then spoon off the fat from roasting pan and discard. Set the pan over two burners. Add the water or wine and bring to a boil, scraping up any brown bits from the bottom with a wooden spoon. Boil until the liquid is reduced by half, about 3 minutes. Pour the contents of the pan into the stockpot.

3. Add enough water to the stockpot to cover the bones and vegetables by 2 inches (about 6 quarts). Bring to just under a boil, then reduce the heat to a bare simmer (bubbles should just gently break at the surface). Add the herbs and peppercorns and very gently simmer, uncovered, over low heat for 8 hours, adding more water as necessary to keep everything submerged.

4. Pass the stock through a cheesecloth-lined sieve (do not press on the solids) into a large heatproof bowl or another stockpot; discard the solids. Season with the salt. The stock will be dark brown. Skim off fat if using immediately or let cool completely (in an ice water bath, if desired) before transferring to airtight containers. Refrigerate at least 8 hours to allow the fat to accumulate at the top; lift off and discard the fat before using or storing. (Stock can be refrigerated in an airtight container up to 1 week, or frozen up to 6 months.)

Homemade Chicken Stock

MAKES 2½ QUARTS

5   pounds assorted chicken parts (backs, necks, legs, and wings), rinsed

2   medium carrots, peeled and chopped into 2-inch lengths

2   celery stalks, chopped into 2-inch lengths

2   medium onions, peeled and cut into quarters

1   or 2 dried bay leaves

1   teaspoon whole black peppercorns

1½   teaspoons kosher salt

1. Place the chicken parts in a stockpot just large enough to hold them with about 3 inches of room above (an 8-quart pot should do) and add enough water to cover by 1 inch (about 3 quarts). Bring to a boil over medium-high heat, using a ladle to skim impurities and fat that rise to the top.

2. Add the vegetables, bay leaf (as desired), and peppercorns and reduce the heat to a bare simmer (bubbles should just gently break the surface). Cook, skimming frequently, for at least 1½ hours and up to 4 hours.

3. Pass the stock through a cheesecloth-lined sieve into a large heatproof measuring cup or another bowl or pot. (Do not press on the solids; discard them.) Stir in the salt.

4. Skim off the fat if using immediately, or let the stock cool completely (in an ice bath, if desired) before transferring to airtight containers. Refrigerate at least 8 hours to allow the fat to accumulate at the top; lift off and discard the fat before using or storing the stock. (Stock can be refrigerated in an airtight container up to 1 week, or frozen up to 6 months.)

Homemade Turkey Stock

MAKES 5 CUPS

  Neck and heart from a 14- to 16-pound turkey, and/or 1 pound turkey wings

1   large onion, peeled and halved

1   medium carrot, peeled and cut into 2-inch lengths

1   celery stalk, cut into 2-inch lengths

  Small handful of parsley sprigs and stems

1   dried bay leaf

5   whole black peppercorns

1. Place all the ingredients in a large stockpot. Add 10 cups cold water and bring to a boil over medium-high heat. Reduce the heat to a simmer and cook until reduced by half, about 1 hour, skimming any impurities that rise to the top.

2. Pass the stock through a cheesecloth-lined sieve into a heatproof bowl; discard solids. If not using immediately, let the stock cool before transferring it to an airtight container. (Stock can be refrigerated in an airtight container up to 1 week, or frozen up to 6 months.)

Homemade Vegetable Stock

MAKES 2 QUARTS

1   tablespoon olive oil
1   large onion, peeled, half coarsely chopped, the other half kept whole
2   large celery stalks, sliced ½ inch thick
2   medium carrots, unpeeled and sliced ½ inch thick
2   garlic cloves, thinly sliced
8   flat-leaf parsley sprigs
8   basil sprigs
4   thyme sprigs
2   dried bay leaves
¼   teaspoon whole black peppercorns
    Kosher salt and freshly ground pepper

1. Brown the vegetables: Heat the oil in a medium stockpot over medium until hot but not smoking. Add the chopped onion and cook, stirring often, until beginning to brown, 10 to 15 minutes. Add the celery, carrots, and garlic and cook, stirring occasionally, until the vegetables are tender and lightly browned, about 10 minutes.

2. Make the stock: Pour in enough water to cover the vegetables by 1 inch (8 to 10 cups) and add the herbs, peppercorns, and remaining half onion. Bring to a boil. Reduce the heat to maintain a gentle simmer and cook, uncovered, 1 hour.

3. Strain the stock: Pour the stock through a fine-mesh sieve into a large bowl or another pot, pressing on the vegetables to extract as much flavorful liquid as possible. (Discard any solids.) Season with 1½ teaspoons salt and ¼ teaspoon pepper. If not using immediately, cool in an ice bath before transferring to airtight containers. (Stock can be refrigerated in an airtight container up to 1 week, or frozen up to 6 months.)

Pâte Brisée

MAKES ENOUGH FOR ONE 9-INCH
DOUBLE-CRUST PIE, OR ONE 10½-BY-15¼-INCH
SINGLE-CRUST PIE

2½   cups unbleached all-purpose flour
1   teaspoon sugar
1   teaspoon table salt
2   sticks (1 cup) cold unsalted butter, cut into small pieces
7   to 8 tablespoons ice water

1. Pulse the flour, sugar, and salt in a food processor until combined.

2. Add the butter and pulse until the mixture resembles coarse meal with some pea-size pieces remaining.

3. Drizzle 5 tablespoons ice water over the mixture; pulse several times to combine. Add more water, 1 tablespoon at a time, and pulse until the mixture holds together when pinched.

4. For a 9-inch pie, shape dough into 2 disks and wrap each in plastic. Refrigerate for at least 1 hour and up to 1 day before using. For a single crust, like the Apple Crumb Pie (page 278), shape the dough into 1 disk and wrap in plastic. Refrigerate for at least 1 hour and up to 1 day before using.

Whipped Cream

MAKES 2 CUPS

1   cup cold heavy cream
2   tablespoons confectioners' sugar, or to taste

In a chilled medium bowl, whisk the cream with an electric mixer on medium speed until soft peaks form, about 3 minutes. Add the confectioners' sugar and whisk until stiff peaks form, about 2 minutes more.

MARTHA'S NOTE

To avoid creating water pockets in the pâte brisée, be sure to strain the ice out of the water before drizzling it in and processing.

Puff Pastry

MAKES 2 POUNDS 11 OUNCES

4 sticks (2 cups) cold unsalted butter, cut into small pieces

1 pound (about 3¼ cups) unbleached all-purpose flour, plus more for dusting

2½ teaspoons table salt

1¼ to 1½ cups heavy cream

1. In a stand mixer fitted with the paddle attachment, beat the butter until smooth. Add ½ cup flour. Mix until smooth. Scrape this dough into a flat square about 1 inch thick. The square should measure about 5 inches by 5 inches. Wrap well in plastic and chill for at least 30 minutes.

2. In a large bowl, combine the remaining flour with the salt. Gradually add the cream and mix until a rough dough is formed; it should not be sticky. Do not overmix. Roll the dough into a rectangle, about 12 inches by 7 inches. Wrap well in plastic, and chill for at least 30 minutes.

3. Remove the flour dough from the refrigerator and place on a lightly floured work surface. Place the chilled butter square at the bottom edge of the rectangle and fold the flour dough over to completely encase the butter, sealing the edges by pinching them together and forming tight hospital corners at the edges. Wrap well in plastic, and chill for at least 30 minutes.

4. Remove the dough from the refrigerator. On a lightly floured board, gently pound the dough all over in regular intervals with a rolling pin. Working in only one direction (lengthwise), gently roll the dough into a 20-by-9-inch rectangle, squaring corners with a bench scraper and your hands as you go. Using a dry pastry brush, sweep off excess flour. With a short side

facing you, fold the rectangle in thirds like a business letter, aligning the edges carefully and keeping each edge square. Turn the dough a quarter-turn clockwise, so the flap opening faces right, like a book. This completes the first turn.

5. Pound across the dough, again in regular intervals, and roll out again to a 20-by-9-inch rectangle, rolling in the same lengthwise direction. Fold the dough again into thirds. This completes the second turn. Wrap the dough in plastic and refrigerate until well chilled, about 1 hour.

6. Repeat the rolling, turning, and chilling process for a total of six turns; always start each turn with the opening of the dough to the right, and always make your trifold in the same manner, that is, by starting from either the top of the dough or the bottom each time. By the sixth and final turn, the dough should be very smooth, with no lumps of butter visible. Use as little flour as possible for the rolling and brush off any excess before folding the dough. If the dough becomes too elastic or too warm to work with, return it to the refrigerator until firm.

7. Wrap the finished dough in plastic and refrigerate until ready to use, at least 2 hours after your final turn, or freeze for future use.

MARTHA'S NOTE

Make small indentations in the dough at the end of each turn so you won't lose track of how many rotations you've finished.

RESOURCES

The following is a list of the trusted vendors and providers included in this book.

Balthazar for delicious bread. *balthazarny.com*

Barney Greengrass for smoked salmon and herring. *barneygreengrass.com*

Black Diamond for quality caviar. *blackdiamondcaviarnyc.com*

Breads Bakery for lovely baked goods. *breadsbakery.com*

Copps Island Oysters is our local supplier of fresh oysters in shell or shucked. *coppsislandoysters.com*

Eataly for fresh vegetables and fruits, salad greens, dried pastas, olive oils, and Italian cheeses. *eataly.com*

Fourth Creek Food Co. for red-pepper relish. *fourthcreekfoods.com*

Frog Hollow Farm for fresh-picked stone fruits. *froghollow.com*

Hemlock Hill Farm & Market for fresh meat and poultry. *hemlockhillfarm.com*

Kalustyan's for grains, spices, and pantry items. *foodsofnations.com*

Katagiri Japanese Grocery for all Asian ingredients. *katagiri.com*

République Café & Bakery for brioche loaves. *republiquela.com*

LMNOP Bakery is my local artisan baker in Katonah, New York. *lmnopbakery.com*

Mister Spear is a California grower of artichokes and asparagus. *misterspear.com*

Mt. Kisco Seafood is my local fishmonger. *mtkiscoseafood.com*

Murray's Cheese for excellent imported cheeses and pastas. *murrayscheese.com*

Pat LaFrieda Meat Purveyors is my favorite butcher for prime meats. *lafrieda.com*

Russ & Daughters for smoked salmon, cream cheese, dried fruits, and dried mushrooms. *russanddaughters.com*

Urbani Truffles for the best truffles. *urbani.com*

Vertical Bay Maine is a wonderful Maine grower of scallops. *verticalbaymaine.com*

Pantry Staples

Below is a list of my everyday supplies.

Butter: Vermont Creamery

Buttermilk: Kate's

Crème fraîche: Vermont Creamery

Dijon mustard: Maille

Flour: Heckers

Kosher salt: Diamond Crystal

Mayonnaise: Hellmann's

Puff pastry dough: LeCoq Cuisine

Yogurt starter: The White Moustache

FAVORITE TOOLS

Here is a very small *batterie de cuisine* list of favorite, sometimes-hard-to-find tools. These items are my kitchen essentials I have discovered on my travels and in the hundreds of small grocery stores and specialty markets I love to visit.

1. Square Ladle

We developed this clever stainless-steel tool for my Martha Stewart collection, and I find myself reaching for it quite regularly. Its flat edges make it perfect for skimming the foam from stock or for scraping the sides of a pot to get the very last drop of sauce. The corners act like little spouts, so you don't spill when transferring hot liquids to small bowls or delicious jam to jars.

2. Sesame Seed Roaster

Whenever I travel, I search out unique local tools. I found this smart and charming long-handled roaster in Japan; but it's also available in specialty-food markets and online. To use it, scoop sesame seeds into the wire-mesh basket and gently shake it over a flame to bring out their nutty flavor. Because you're holding it in your hand, you can control the heat and browning better than if stirring the seeds in a hot pan. Stop before they're done and spread them on a towel, as they'll continue to brown as they cool. This tool can also be used to roast spices and nuts.

3. Rasp Graters

A **long, flat rasp grater** is simply the best tool for creating light, airy piles of fine citrus zest or Parmesan or other hard cheese. I also use it when I want fresh garlic or ginger so fine it's almost a paste. I like to grate with the channel of the rasp turned upward, collecting the zest as I go so I can drop it right where I need it—it's a good thing!

A **paddle-shaped cheese grate**r is a similar tool with slightly coarser—but just as beautifully sharp—teeth, for hard cheeses or even chocolate.

4. Truffle Shaver

When preparing truffles, it's essential to slice them as thin as possible, so this traditional tool is a worthy investment. When selecting one, the key things to look for are a razor-sharp blade and ease of handling. My handheld shaver creates the finest, papery-thin shavings of raw truffle, which are then perfect to shower over a pasta dish, risotto, or a warm egg, enhancing the flavor and aroma of a dish.

5. Rolling Pin

As a lifelong baker and pastry maker, I have a special fondness for rolling pins. I'm always finding a new interesting one to add to my already very large collection. A rolling pin should be well balanced and smooth and have handles that are comfortable to hold. Take good care of it and it will last a lifetime. Simply dust it with flour to prevent sticking and clean with a damp cloth.

6. Pastry Wheel Cutter

For precisely cut pastry, a cutter with a rotating wheel is very efficient, especially when used with a ruler as a guide. I often use pastry wheel cutters with fluted edges to create a decorative edge on strips of pastry.

7. Muddler

You can find this classic bartender's tool in hardwoods like birch, walnut, or cherry, as well as sterling silver, stainless steel, plastic, and bamboo. It's used like a long pestle to gently mix and bruise herbs and fruits to bring out their essence. I also use it to mash up the ingredients for Caesar dressing.

8. Shellfish Knives

A good, sturdy **oyster knife** is the epitome of the right tool for the job. Its wide, short blade is made of strong steel, with a pointed end made for pushing through the hinge of the shell. It works well for shucking sea scallops, too.

The **clam knife** is similar, but its blade is longer and thinner, as shucking clam shells is more of a wedge-and-pry operation. You can find lovely, wooden-handled shellfish knives, but I prefer these professional-quality versions that put function first: They get washed a lot, so plastic handles just make sense.

9. Kunz Spoon

Most every professional chef or test-kitchen cook I know has at least one of these utensils by their stove. Originally designed by chef Gray Kunz, who ran the kitchen at an excellent restaurant in New York City called Lespinasse, this spoon is the perfect size and shape and weight for so many tasks, from stirring, to saucing, to dolloping whipped cream onto dessert.

10. Ginger Grater

This ceramic grater is a traditional tool used in Japan and is worth picking up. Its teeth stay sharp for ages and do a beautiful job of shredding fresh ginger and separating out those stringy fibers. Use a stiff brush to clean it.

11. Spider

A traditional spider strainer, with a bamboo handle and wire-mesh basket, is useful for so many things; I keep several in my kitchen. It's designed for retrieving deep-fried foods out of hot oil, but I use it instead for scooping everything from vegetables to pasta.

12. Brushes

I always have at least two pastry brushes nearby when I'm baking—one for wet tasks like brushing an egg wash onto a pie crust; and one for dry, such as sweeping away excess flour. Best-quality natural-bristle brushes won't shed as you work and will soak up your glaze or coating and spread it evenly.

13. Flexible Spatula

Wood-handled spatulas with flexible, silicone heads are workhorses in my kitchen. I use them to stir batters, fold in ingredients, and scrape the sides of bowls or pots. Silicone is heat-resistant and won't scratch cooking surfaces, and the wood handles don't conduct heat or chemically react with acidic food.

ACKNOWLEDGMENTS

Thank you to the extraordinary team who helped me create my one hundredth book:

Photography
Carlo Barreto
Dana Gallagher
Alexei Topounov

Food Team
Frances Boswell
Sarah Carey
Sarah Comerford Loria
Cynthia Gasparre
Thomas Joseph
Jeff Srole

Prop Styling
Lisa Wagner

Design and Editorial
James Maikowski
Susanne Ruppert

Bedford Team
Dorian Arrich
Heather Kirkland
Matt Krack
Ryan McCallister
Josefa Palacio
Elvira Rojas
Enma Sandoval
Jocelyn Santos

Special Thanks to
Kim Dumer
Ryan Mesina
Kevin Sharkey
Daisy Toye

Clarkson Potter
Marquee Brands

Thank you to the many talented food editors, recipe developers, testers, and support staff who have worked in the kitchens at Martha Stewart Living Omnimedia over the years.

Jennifer Aaronson
Christine Albano
Judy Lockhart Allen
Sara Backhouse
John Barricelli
Cindy Bearman
Tara Bench
Shira Bocar
Frances Boswell
Stephana Bottom
Caitlin Haught Brown
Monita Buchwald
Sarah Carey
Abigail Chipley
Allison Lewis Clapp
Elizabeth Colling
Samantha Connell
Kristen Evans
Emma Feigenbaum
Yolanda Florez
Amy Gropp Forbes
Sandra Rose Gluck
Allison Hedges
Lauren Higgins
Kirk C. Hunter
Khalil Hymore
Aida Ibarra
Thomas Joseph
Shelly Kaldunski
Wendy Kalen
Anna Kovel
Wendy Kromer
Kristina Kurek
Lindsay Leopold
Greg Lofts
Charlotte March
Charlyne Mattox
Heather Meldrom
Denise Mickelsen
Carla Lalli Music
Sara Neumeier
Claire Perez
Dawn Perry
Melissa Perry
Elizabeth Pilar
Gertrude Porter
Lori Powell
Lucinda Scala Quinn
Laura Rege
Susan Hanemann Rogol
Jason Schreiber
Samantha Seneviratne
Susan Streit Sherman
Wendy Sidewater
Susan Spungen
Heidi Johannsen Stewart
Lesley Stockton
Susan Sugarman
Susan Testa
Kavita Thirupuvanam
Lauryn Tyrell
Molly Wenk
Brittany Williams
Avery Wittkamp
Riley Wofford
Caroline Wright

INDEX

Martha